"Lisa DeLong's achingly beautiful story of life, love, and loss is a very personal and powerful journey. We have been friends for over a decade, and her son Justin was one of my heroes. Lisa's son Jacob, who is also one of my heroes, has been at war with the disease that took his brother's life. *Blood Brothers* is a real life experience of hope, compassion, and faith. Once you meet this mother and her family, your life will change forever."

—Kathy Ireland, CEO Kathy Ireland Worldwide

Dear Caren,

Blood
BROTHERS

Thank you for
sharing wellness with
others.

Much love,
Lisi
5/2019

LISA SOLIS DELONG

Blood
BROTHERS

*a memoir of faith and loss
while raising two sons with cancer*

Edited by Amanda Reese
Cover design by Amber Gulilat
Interior design by Nathan Harmony

Published in the United States of America
ISBN: 978-1-61777-152-1
Biography & Autobiography / Personal Memoirs / Cancer
11.09.29

Dedication

Just about everything I've done for the past four years has been dedicated to keeping Jacob alive. This book is for Justin who prepared the way, for Jessica and Joelle, who have had to stand by and watch. To Jacob, who probably won't remember what all the fuss was about; and to David, who knows as intimately as I do this life of loss, as only a loving father can.

Acknowledgments

I have never done this before, written an acknowledgment piece for a book; and it is much tougher than I thought—not because I don't know what to say but because there are so many kind people to say things about. I am more experienced at being a housewife, mother, sister, and nurse than I am at being a writer. So it is with a grateful heart that I share the names of people here, whom, if you were like me, you would be blessed to meet one day.

Four years ago, a community surrounded my family and me when I had to stop working in order to take care of my youngest son. Many of these folks felt kicked in the gut too when we had to face leukemia again because they knew our first son, Justin, when he fought his illness, and they have suffered right alongside us. They are proud Santa Claritans, many of them teachers and coaches from Canyon High School, who put together a fundraising event and called it the "Jakie Jog," where thousands of people from all over the country rallied to raise so much money that I have been able to stay home and thus discover that I am a writer. If not for their gift, I would not have been able to squeeze in the work of writing in-between all of the care giving.

If my friend Steve Gold had not come over one night, sat me down, and told me to take a look at the numbers—the amount of lost wages, increased medical expenses, and needs of a growing family of five—none of the words you are about to read would have made it past my journal, which I started long before Justin's illness and his death, because that is what I do when I am stressed.

A lot of people contributed to keeping us afloat. If I wrote them all, it would be a book in itself. So here is a list of several people who made it happen: Steve, Kathy and Stevie Gold, George Velarde, Paul Broneer, Chris Jackson, Kathy Patterson, Debbie Habberstad, and hundreds of others who scooped up our family in their net of generosity. To all of you, this is my official thank-you note, the one I wanted to send when my life was falling apart but could not.

There are several people who were total strangers but upon meeting made me feel like old friends. You'll understand why I owe them my gratitude when you read about them in my story: Jim Etzel, Kathy Ireland, Tony Potts, Pete Carroll, Angelica Logan, Debbie Kester, and Richard Pearce.

Justin had a lot of friends; Josh Relles was his childhood pal. Josh Bush and Leanne Riggin were as well; and although they were only in their teens, they acted with more courage than most adults in staying close to their friend. For that you will not be forgotten.

And then there are the medical staff, who make a decision to work long, long, thankless hours to keep children alive and who, I know from experience, struggle to keep a stiff upper lip in the face of life's most extreme tragedies every day: Dr. Judy Sato and Dr. Arcenue of City of Hope and their team, who tried their best to save Justin's life. Your efforts remain a source of comfort. Dr. Stuart Siegel and Dr. David Tishler of Childrens Hospital Los Angeles. Nurses Susan, Chris, Maria, especially Kathy M. and Dee, who were there for both boys. Physician's assistant Jed, thank you for making Jacob laugh and always knowing what to do when I did not. To medical social worker Karla Garcia and the entire Childrens Hospital Los

Angeles team, from the valet parking attendants to the physicians—thank you and please, please keep up the good work. Dr. May Tang and Dr. Peter Kim of Facey Medical Group, thank you for making the process that much easier.

There are those people who were my friends before I became the mother of two boys with cancer and have chosen to stick with me even when, as my friend Jim says, I have had to eat another shit sandwich, and it has been painful for them to watch. Thank you for helping me to come out smelling like a rose: Donna and Randy Relles, Dave and Yesenia Hickman, and Mike and Cherie McGregor.

To Pastor Jim Ryan and the entire church family at Heart of the Canyons, including Carol Ryan, Ted and Tracy Grissom, Stephanie Waite, Diane Briones, Stacy Gall, and Connie Rice, where I have shown up late for twenty years, served little to none in the last decade, and still receive smiles and hugs when I show up.

To the Michael Hoefflin Foundation for Children's Cancer team, sometimes it is hard to believe that I have had two kids with cancer until I gather with you and see myself in your midst. I have learned so much from the families you serve, the ones you care so much about and work so diligently to support. Thank you for introducing me to Elizabeth Hill, who empowered me before she left, and David Hatfield, who taught me that a child can endure intense suffering and still exude concern for others far better than grown-ups can. Sometimes the purest of souls are assigned the most difficult tasks to show us what real love is.

And then there is my natural family, who, in my way of thinking, has had no choice but to stick with me because that's what Mom and Dad taught us *familia* does. Still, they deserve my deepest gratitude, because some families can't do this. You have stayed close and done so with love and good humor. My *hermana*, Lori Powers, who, among other things, has shared her artistic talents with Jacob as his teacher but most memorably designed Justin's gravestone and immortalized him for me by painting his portrait.

To Mike, her husband, who has not only babysat my children but done a better job of it than we did at times. Their children—Devin, Leah, and Lauren, who was born six days after Justin and whom I'm glad to have so I can put my arms around her and imagine what life would have been like had she and Justin lived it out together. You have done him proud. My little sister in Texas, Cathie Crowell, thank you for loving Jacob as your own. And to her husband, Mike, and their kids, Mikala, Emily, and little Isaiah. It is comforting to know you can be counted on whenever Jacob needs to feel an extra dose of cousins' love. My big brother, Ken Solis, who would have laid down his life for Justin and has always been available to fix our broken stuff; and his wife, Deborah, for bringing joy to my brother. My big brother, Rick Solis, the oldest of us five, who paved the way for all of us. His wife, Maria, and their children—Kristina, Andrew, and Sarah—thanks for making time to babysit, fix technological problems, and helping out your auntie. And to my parents, Richard and Shirley Solis, who showed me by example what it is to love a family. I miss you, Dad.

And I would be remiss to ignore my married family, the DeLongs, who love with an unconditional, generous, never-ending kind of love because their mother, Betty DeLong Hoffman, and father, Ed DeLong, showed them how. Ed, Linda and Ron Frasier, Randy Bittle, and Denise Cobos, thank you for offering the same to me. Betty, you are missed.

I have discovered that most writers don't become writers alone. I have had the privilege of meeting and learning from wise teachers: Floyd Moose at College of the Canyons, who taught me the difference between a personal essay and a memoir, and Jennie Nash and Barbara Abercrombie at UCLA Writer's Extension, who not only taught me how to craft words but always treated me like I belonged. Thanks. I needed that.

I want to include another teacher here who, although I did not take a class with him, read my manuscript back in 2006 and inspired me to take writing seriously. Thank you, Marko (Mark Hand).

To Joe Loya, who re-entered my life after a thirty-three-year absence via Facebook at the most opportune time and generously shared his expertise with me. Your wit and laughter encouraged me during the editing phase. Thank you for including me as a fellow writer.

To the Last Sunday Writers, with whom I meet once a month. Your critical eye has served to pull me out of the mud while working on several of the chapters here, and your enthusiasm for all of our work has kept me pecking at the keys.

There are people who extended their personal gifts to Jacob and I over and over again in recent years, including Mona Hoffman, who saved my life many times by taking care of Jacob even if it was the middle of the night and he was ill. Her expertise as a NICU and PICU nurse were invaluable to me. Dr. Mary Smith, who started out volunteering to tutor Jacob in reading but fell in love with him and decided she would rather just play with him "because that is more fun." Hugo Cherre, whom we appreciate for the three years of gymnastics lessons he gave Jacob without letting me pay him a cent. Lance Willis who made the photos here possible, thanks for the tech support.

There are people who extended practical services to our family above and beyond the ordinary. United Oil, AIM Landscape, Vons. com, and A. Allbright Paint, thank you for making our lives easier.

I would be disappointed in myself if I left out young Ryan Starke, Jacob's best friend. They first met in preschool at the age of three where they laughed like hyenas whenever they were together. Thank you for making me laugh too. Sam, his big brother, whom I swear I'm gonna write a book entitled *Sam Said* someday based on his critical advice on everything from shaving your legs to where babies come from.

Now, about my high school sweetheart, David, who braved the cancer course by my side with courage and love for our children, who's "Just do the best you can" mentality has both calmed me and frustrated me at times over our twenty-seven years of marriage. There is no one on earth who shares the joy and sorrow of our two boys more deeply than him. I could not have chosen a better partner.

Acknowledging my children feels like I am giving them a graduation card, which I guess is fitting since they have been schooled in the college of dark knowledge and have no diploma to show for it. Consider this your commencement. To Jessica, the big sister who became the oldest in our family by default and took on the task with courage, please know the welling pride I have for you and your work in Young Life ministries and how much I enjoy your spitfire personality. Justin would have loved how you turned out. To Joelle, the little sister who became the big sister when one brother left and another came, you amaze me the way you take care of Jacob so instinctively and fearlessly and how, through it all, you have remained honest with yourself and focused on your future. And to Jacob, thank you for teaching me how brothers are bonded by more than mere blood. To Justin, you know how much I still talk to you. Thank you for being willing to come and teach me about life and death and faith and for leaving me with so many wonderful memories to hold on to.

Table of Contents

Your Heart Will Rejoice?

The new gravestone stood out like a seashell on a lonesome beach. The morning sun reflected off of its polished marble surface. I swallowed hard; pulled my youngest son, Jacob, tight; and came closer. Flags, large and small, waved as if to greet us. Jacob's brown hair blew across his forehead. He winced but did not cry. It was a steep slope, and I had trouble navigating with him on my hip. After a deep breath, I stepped with care over one grave after another. A metallic sound came from two Mylar balloons tethered by an angel on a child's grave. There on this wind-whipped hillside, under a lurching oak sapling, the body of my firstborn lay beneath the sprinklers and the sod. Standing at his grave, gravity prevailed as my eyes read the words we had chosen:

Lisa Solis DeLong

Justin David DeLong
7/3/85–7/15/2000
Such a great kid … Such a great smile.

"Therefore you too now have sorrow; but I will see you again, and your heart will rejoice, and no one takes your joy away from you," (John 16:22 NAS).

I wrestled as much with the archaic words left behind by the one most known for his suffering, as with an impatient Jacob who wanted down. I lowered him on to the cold, stone surface which appeared to have little effect on him as it met the bottom of his tender soles. He was too young to know that this was where his brother lay, too innocent to weep at a moment like this. But I was not. In an instant, tears sprinkled the etched stone. Justin was too young to be there. His name more reminiscent of a pop star. Fifteen was too soon.

I came because it had been too long. My son's grave should not have gone unmarked for nearly four months with nothing but a numbered metal tag and a mismatched patch of sod. I couldn't convince my husband or two daughters to come with me that day. Seeing Justin's grave was more than their beleaguered emotions could handle, unlike Jacob, the youngest and just a toddler. He had no choice but to stay by my side. Even if he had, he probably would have chosen to be with me anyway. Toddlers are like that about their mommies.

Tears splattered the front of my shirt. The wind caught them and threw them back at me. My head felt heavy, as though it were filled with wet sand. Dropping to my knees, I pressed my fingertips along the clean, sharp edges of every letter. As Jacob toddled close by, the tips of my probing fingers worked to convince my mind and, in turn, persuade my heart that Justin's death was true.

I didn't know how to live like this, without my Justin, without joy personified, his positive attitude, his constant smile, his good-natured kindness. I know that this portrayal sounds like a cliché; the kind of sugar-coated adulation one hears at graveside gatherings even if the dead guy was a jerk; but ask anyone who knew Justin and they would agree with my description. At that moment, even with little Jacob at my side, from where I stood, joy was in a casket; and with this much pain, I wasn't sure it could ever be resurrected. The thought of it wearied me.

I hated coming here. It was always windy. It could be still as stones at home, and here, just six miles away, an unceasing whipping and lashing of air pounded the Southern California hillside cemetery known as Eternal Valley. Overlooking the frenzied 14 Freeway, Eternal Valley's steep slopes held bent trees down below, hunched over like old men disfigured by at least fifty years of wind. Up here, at Justin's grave, it was too contemporary. The unceasing roar of traffic was irritating. I wished it were the ocean.

Jacob wobbled nearby and picked a rainbow pinwheel from a neighboring grave. It spun faster as he lifted it in triumph. He was much more adventurous than his brother had been at this age. I worried that I would not be able to keep up with him. I lowered my head, realizing that he would never remember seeing the radiance of Justin's giant smile or recall the sound of his goofy giggle. He would have no memory of being held in the strength of Justin's teenage arms. Because of this quirk of fate, Jacob would never know the pain of living without him the way I did. I felt a sense of relief for his lack of memories. I wrapped myself in mine like a blanket, wool lined with satin, uncomfortable on one side, soothing on the other.

I lifted my eyes to the horizon, my back to the blows of the wind, longing for a holy glimpse of some kind, something to prove that Justin's death was not the end and that I could somehow feel the same glow that I had felt with him alive. I recalled meeting a woman once whose young son, just days before he died, had seen Jesus in the clouds. That experience calmed her after his death. I thought about another mother I'd met who had held a wild dove in her hand after her daughter's funeral. The experience reassured her that her daughter was still near. I'd had spiritual experiences, lots of them, but I didn't understand them yet.

I had believed in everlasting life and in the existence of heaven from an early age, but that was before I knew what death was. No one really knows death until you live with absence. Without Justin's voice, his touch, and the scent of his hair, first for one day and then one week, I started to understand; then after one month, then four, my mind began to comprehend what it meant for Justin to be gone. Seeing his gravestone forced the reality deep. It was one thing to believe in heaven, when no one I loved this much was there, and a whole other thing to trust that heaven was real and that my child lived there. Where was it? Did he miss me? In that moment, all I could do was weep and beg God to show me Justin. *If he is in the wind, surely I could feel him pass through me.* All I felt was air.

My fingers trembled as they lifted from his name and then followed the edges of the designs we'd created for the stone: a golf club and unlaced running shoes. I read the words over and over again as I replayed his last days. The end had come without warning, just as the beginning had. The fear of losing Justin began in 1990, when he was first diagnosed with acute lymphoblastic leukemia at the age of five. After he relapsed nearly ten years later, I realized that fear. And now here I was, at the foot of his grave, challenging him to comfort me in the aftermath of every mother's biggest nightmare. It was one thing to trust God's help in the fight for life. It was an entirely different matter when life was over.

The trees near Justin's grave were young and small, unlike the ones down below at the base of the hill, in the older part of the cemetery. Down there, near the entrance, the trees were giants: pines and oaks. They swayed at the incessant wind, established, rooted, and immoveable. My faith was once like that. But now it was Justin I needed. I had held him in my arms, nursed him at my breast, and raised him to young adulthood with the best of my energies. Jesus, whom I had invested myself in as well, felt more a myth than a man. For the first time in my journey as a believer, I had trouble believing.

Jacob plopped himself next to a marker several gravesites over to pet a fuzzy, plastic puppy left behind by previous visitors. Its head nodded in obedience to the wind. Lilies in metal vases arched and held onto their stems. I looked across the wide expanse of green lawn to find we were the only ones there, and again I lowered my heavy head and sobbed. I heard the distant "caw caw," of circling crows and raised my eyes.

In no time, Jacob had traveled too far up the hill. *Justin never would have ventured that far at this age. The girls yes, but not him.* He had not been one to leave my side. Lost in memories, my battered maternal instincts flickered, and I managed a response. I called to Jacob to come back, but my voice was blown downwind. I stood up and gestured for him to come to me.

"Come back to Mommy!" I yelled.

He turned, spied a "Happy Birthday" balloon dancing before him, and snatched it up. Heading straight for me, picking up speed like a runaway freight train, arms loaded with confiscated trinkets, trampling over stones marked, "Beloved," and, "Precious," he smiled and drew uncontrollably closer. I lowered myself to catch him. Releasing his treasures on top of me and his brother's stone, he wrapped his soft, thick arms around me and squealed, "Mommy!" knocking me backward onto the grass. He kissed me strongly. I laughed out loud. It seemed to be the wrong place for laughter, but I couldn't help it.

We cuddled on the grass for a moment, and I felt a lightness of heart that had been absent for months. It showed up that fast. Perhaps joy had not left me forever after all? Pulling Jacob onto my lap, I told him, "You are like good medicine." He leaned into me, contented. I nicknamed him that day, saying, "You are my little medicine man." For his touch and his laughter cured me if only for a moment, staving off the pain like the finest of analgesics. We sat for a while, my arms soothed by the warmth of his body, my lips consoling themselves on his soft brow.

My head was not as heavy, and my arms felt lighter. I looked out toward the bustling freeway at the passing cars rushing north and south driven by people seemingly indifferent to the dead bodies buried there. I wondered if I would ever be that liberated again, free to pass by without so much as a glimpse in death's direction.

We stood for a moment as I let the blood flow return to my numb legs, and then Jacob and I turned and walked up the hill, his hand in mine. I returned the trinkets to their owners as best I could, without worry that anyone could have tattled if I got it wrong. We approached the car, and I picked him up. I held him close as the ends of our hair whipped at our eyes. In a blink, we were on our way home.

Freeway Dream

I used to wake up a bit baffled by a recurring dream. I couldn't tell you exactly how old I was when it started, but I have had it most of my adult life. It always began the same way. I was driving along a busy freeway with the usual array of motor vehicles in the flow of traffic. A pickup truck with an ATV strapped down in the back sped by, followed by a faded Camaro, the gray-haired driver focused straight ahead as a yellow convertible with a man and a woman wearing visors laughed and tossed their heads back, lost in a moment of light-hearted gaiety. There were minivans and SUVs full of families going the usual places: soccer practice, church, or perhaps a school function; boys and girls giggled and poked each other in the backseats. Through it all, a couple of spirited motorcyclists straddled crotch rockets and wove their way through traffic like ballistic missiles, their quick, explosive movement carefree and reckless.

I had never been able to tell what kind of car I was driving in my dream. I guess it really didn't matter. I was comfortable, and I had a clear view of what was going on around me. After I drove for a while, the flow of traffic slowed. Red taillights flickered and began to fill like red blood cells clogging an artery.

Each time the traffic flow slowed, it became evident that a horrifying accident had taken place. Cars were strewn everywhere. I dodged the congestion as breaks screeched and cars came to a sudden, crashing halt. A semi truck rested on its side. Gasoline bled from its tank as gray smoke rose from the engine. I was able to keep going through the debris. Sports cars were tossed like June bugs stuck on their backs; minivans crumpled; SUVs were surrounded by broken glass, kids' backpacks, and a soccer ball or two. Alienated bumpers were strewn between injured motorists who reached out their side-lying windows. Bloodied and broken, they looked at me as I passed by in a state of cautious calm. I observed a motorcycle or two strewn across the asphalt, their passengers spread about with limbs bent in awkward positions. Some of the accident victims were alive, and some appeared to be dead. I never panicked in my dream. I just looked at them and nodded as if I knew them. I understood that I was supposed to be there. Our gaze was somehow comforting. They reached with outstretched arms covered in asphalt-blackened abrasions. We looked eye to eye, except for the dead. Their eyes were dull and hazy or closed. They were never lying there alone. They were held by people who appeared to love them. There were many others who were injured. The scene continued until I got past the congestion and the debris dwindled, and then I came to a clearing where the freeway was empty and open and endless. In my dream, I never crashed.

In no way were these dreams nightmares, although to some they could have been. I was not afraid in my dream. I didn't wake up sweating, heart pounding out of my chest, or short of breath. I just woke up wondering what it all meant. The dream always left me with a sense of familiar dread and well defined purpose. I did not know what this feeling was until I started recognizing it in my real life.

When I became a registered nurse in 1983, I thought that the ailing people whom I was taking care of at LA County Hospital were perhaps the cause of my dream. The diversity of patients varied. The most shocking to me included abandoned drug babies, homeless people with maggot-infested decubitus ulcers, and scores of young men wounded in fights.

One such man was most memorable. He was tone and fit when I admitted him to 9800, the floor where I worked as a new nurse. This was where the gunshots and stabbings ended. He was nineteen, talkative, and upbeat. He knew he'd been shot in a backyard brawl and verbalized awareness that his spinal cord had been severed, but he had not made the connection between that fact and the reality that he would never walk again. He was lying supine in his bed when I walked in with a urinary catheter tray, ready to insert the catheter into his urethra in order to empty his bladder. I was glad he was on his back, because I would have had difficulty moving him. The lower half of his body, which was paralyzed, was like moving sandbags.

"It's time for some relief," I said, setting the tray on the bedside table.

"Yeah. I guess so. I can't feel nothin' down there, but if you say so."

I was twenty years old and uncomfortable with touching a man's genitalia. I tried to remain professional as I opened the tray; draped the patient with a sterile, white, paper sheet; and put on my gloves using sterile technique. As I held his penis in my left hand and swabbed the surface of the urethral orifice with the required antiseptic Betadine swabs, he became aroused. My virgin eyes grew bigger, and so did he, but he showed no hint of embarrassment.

"Look there," he said, grinning. "It still works. See that?"

How could I miss it? I thought and cleared my throat. "Yeah. Okay … um … I'm going to insert the catheter now." I almost said, "This might be uncomfortable," but I realized at the last second how inappropriate that would be. He couldn't feel anything. I had to remind myself that he would never be able to urinate on his own, feel sexual pleasure, or walk. He was practically my age, tall and muscular, every bit a man. It would be a matter of days before his legs would begin to atrophy and his new reality would become unmistakable to him.

I felt changed after meeting this patient. I had witnessed the beginning of one of life's most vital battles: that which lies between the mind and the body. Part of him had died, but his mind had not caught up. Like losing a child, the two components still searched for neurons to touch, like electricity flowing on wires when the wires are cut, the current no longer able to flow. The circuit was not complete. I was this man's nurse for one day, but the memory of him has stayed with me.

Even with all the tragedies I'd seen after being a nurse over the years, I never gave much thought to the meaning behind my recurring dream. I was not freaked out that I had them as many people do. I did, however, wonder what it meant that I didn't die in my dream; I just witnessed death and suffering and kept going. I never imagined that the traumatic scene I'd viewed over and over again in my dream would in many ways mirror the pain, suffering, and death I would experience in real life.

A World We Wanted No Part Of

Dave and I waited within arm's reach of the phone, unable to breathe every time it rang.

"Have you heard anything?"

The news that Justin was sick had circulated, and by 5:00 p.m., we were taking turns answering the phone. These were the days before caller ID and cell phones.

"Nothing yet. Can't talk right now. Please pray that it is just a virus."

Our replies were methodical, distant. I waited in a state of clouded disbelief, replaying the day's events while the word *leukemia* poked at every thought. It had been used to describe the condition of *my* firstborn son, not someone else's. *Mine*. Dave and I remained as focused on Justin as he was on the television screen.

Justin belly-laughed, his head cocked back and a grin across his face. He sat cross-legged in the living room, engrossed in *Mario Brothers*. In 1990, when he was five, the game was a novelty.

"Ha hah," he bellowed. "Take that, Bowser!"

Chewing his tongue frantically, his fingers kept pace as he squeezed the game controller in his small hands.

If only a mother could press pause on time, I'd stop here.

I appreciated the game's distraction. The long, hot August day was supposed to have included a visit to the pediatrician's office for a routine check-up but turned out to be anything but. We had been waiting for several hours when the phone finally rang, and I rushed to answer. It was Dr. V. When I heard the word *leukemia*, it came through the phone and mingled in the air with the arcadelike song of the video game.

"Acute lymphoblastic leukemia," he said. "The most common kind."

Justin had looked a little pale for the past week, and his eyes were swollen when he woke up, but the puffiness went away by midmorning. *Allergies*, I'd thought, and I attributed his pale coloring to the need for more iron in his diet. I had started giving him an increased portion of green, leafy vegetables and a children's daily vitamin. As a registered nurse working on a maternity ward, I had limited experience observing and treating seriously sick kids. Neonates, yes. Kids, no. Justin did not look sick to me, so I didn't give his symptoms much thought, knowing that I would bring them to his doctor's attention when he saw his pediatrician for his kindergarten check-up in just a few days.

When the day of his appointment came, after a breakfast of Cheerios and a banana, I gathered up five-year-old Justin and eighteen-month-old Jessica. It was going to get hot—at least ninety—so I pulled down the window shades and headed out the door. I dropped off Jessica at my friend Donna's house where she could play unrestrained by the confines of the pediatrician's office. Justin and I entered the small waiting room, sat down in the last remaining seat, and turned the pages of *The Cat in the Hat*.

Justin was shy and preferred my lap to the play area in the corner, where kids picked through toys and guarded their newfound treasures. We were placed in an exam room where the posters hanging on the stark, white walls promoted healthy eating habits and the need for vaccinations. I thought, *What a good mother I am. Justin is getting his vaccines on time, and he eats a healthy diet just like the FDA recommends.* The white paper crinkled as we sat close, flipping through *Green Eggs and Ham* on the exam table.

When the door opened, Justin snuggled closer to me as Dr. V entered the room. He was a small, thin man with a thick Indian accent and an unusual sense of humor, the kind that sometimes got him in trouble with the parents of fresh newborns, whose perfect birth plan did not include a saucy little Indian telling them their baby had a big nose.

"Just like his father," he'd say with a chuckle.

I knew him as kindhearted and often misunderstood. I chose him when Justin was born for his reputation as a thorough physician. I'd seen him care for the babies on the women's unit with the zeal of a father, and I respected him for that.

He walked in the exam room, put the chart on the counter by the sink, and started with, "Hello. What is happening, my friend?" Then he turned, took one look at Justin, and spewed, "Oh no, no, no. You nurses, you know how to take care of everyone else but your own kids!"

My eyes filled with tears. Justin was sick, very, very sick.

How could I, his mother, who sees him every day, a medically trained professional, not see how ill he was? I wanted to bang my head against the wall and scream. I don't cry easily, but the tears began to stream down my face.

Doctor V, realizing the lack of sensitivity in his choice of words, softened. "I'm sorry. Kindly let me examine you, Justin," he said.

I slid off the table, helped Justin lie down, and held his hand. His deep brown eyes studied Dr. V's face as the doctor, mumbling and shaking his head, palpated under his jaw, his neck, and then deep into his abdomen. Dr. V was pensive and brisk with his instructions.

"Take Justin to have blood drawn now, please. I will be waiting for you when you are done."

He gathered up Justin's chart and apologized again as I wiped my eyes and left the exam room.

Justin had always been an unusually obedient child. There was never a period of terrible twos. He rarely injured himself, even as an inquisitive toddler, because he rarely ever climbed too high or ran too fast. He was easy, gentle. Even then, when he was faced with a needle penetrating his little arm, he did not scream, kick, or fight. He sat on my lap submissively, flinching as he watched, constantly learning and listening. Waiting for the results was horrible, but Justin didn't know this. He was five, and he was hungry, and he thought eating a turkey sandwich and chips at the café inside the medical building was a treat. He ate while I stared at him, studying his face for signs of illness. All I could see was his pale skin, his full smile, and his sparkling eyes.

Why can't I see whatever it is Dr. V saw?

I concealed the tension and fear in my heart even though the doctor's words played over and over again in my mind.

"More chips?" I asked. "Finish your applesauce," I instructed in an attempt at normalcy.

The results finally came. "Carry them back to Dr. V's office," I was told, so of course I looked at them. I was no expert at pediatric lab results, but I understood immediately that the elevated white blood cell count of fifty-six thousand was well above the normal twenty thousand. I knew these numbers staring back at me were serious, but I couldn't comprehend all that they meant.

This time, Justin and I were directed straight into the doctor's private office. Dr. V sat on the other side of his disheveled desk, where charts were stacked one on top of the other, his dark brows furled, and his face brooding. I wondered how many of those charts held information as potent as my son's. Justin's was at the top of the pile. Dr. V did not make eye contact. He opened Justin's chart and stared at the lab results.

"There is a serious possibility that Justin might have leukemia. I don't know what kind exactly, so we will need to do a bone marrow aspiration test. I have already made arrangements for you to see an oncologist now. Normally, he is closed for lunch. But he will be waiting for you."

His rolling *R*'s and melodic Hindi inflections irritated me as I strained to understand what he was saying.

"Is there any other possible cause for the abnormal lab results?" I questioned.

"It's possible that it might be a virus. Only the bone marrow test will tell."

I didn't cry this time.

"May I use your phone?" I asked with the monotone of a robot. "Donna?" My voice cracked, and my lips began to tremble at the sound of her voice. "Listen, buddy. Can you keep Jessica a little longer?"

"Sure. What's up? Is everything okay?"

Donna was also a registered nurse, and I appreciated her ability to understand what I had to tell her.

"I have some bad news. Dr. V thinks Justin might have leukemia," I said, my voice quivering.

"Oh … no … oh … God … what can I do to help? I'll call Dave for you," she said.

I could hear Jessica giggling in the background, no doubt running around the apartment with Donna's boys, Matthew and Joshua.

"I'd appreciate that, but I don't know how to reach him. He has taken the cross-country team to Lake Pyramid for the day to water ski."

"I'll call your brother, Ken. He'll know what to do."

Donna was the kind of friend who got things done. She was resourceful and quick thinking. She was exactly the person I needed right then. I thanked her, hung up, and left the office feeling a mild sense of irritation at Dave for committing a full day of fun to his team. I was accustomed to being the coach's wife. I'd had fun on many a team-related outing, but right now, I needed *Husband* Dave, not *Coach* Dave. I buckled Justin into his car seat and travelled toward the freeway.

I drove in a state of frozen dread. I kept looking at Justin in his car seat to make sure he was really there, that this was really happening. Arriving at the next doctor's office, I noticed how quiet the building was. There was no hustling and bustling of men, women, or children. It felt foreign. We entered the waiting room where *Reader's Digests* marked tables in the waiting room and were greeted by a doctor whose name I didn't remember. I knew he was an adult oncologist. The office smelled of rubbing alcohol and was bland in color. He told me that this procedure, a bone marrow aspiration, would be difficult and painful for Justin but that anesthesia was not an option. I questioned him but gave in to the urgency in his voice.

"You will have to hold him in the fetal position and not let him move." It was his office's lunch hour, so no one was available to help. I had never seen or assisted with a bone marrow aspiration, and all I could do was pray silent impulses of desperation.

Lord, help me help Justin. Please give me strength. Please give Justin strength.

I was twenty-nine years old, too naïve to know what my options were. However, this much I had learned as a nurse: lie to a child about pain, and you lose their trust forever.

"This is going to hurt," I told him. "But if you lie very still, it will be over more quickly."

He climbed onto the examining table, and I felt weak. He lay on his side, and I placed one hand on his head and one behind his knees and curled him into a ball. As the doctor pushed a large needle into the back of Justin's hip bone, forcing his body to jerk, Justin cried out in pain but did not fight me. He was not a fighter. It was as if he knew what he needed to do. My helpless tears fell on Justin's soft, brown hair as I lowered my head, nearly resting mine on his. Our tears mixed into a puddle.

Sometimes I wonder if this was how Isaac responded to Abraham when he was about to be sacrificed. Did he lay down in total trust like my Justin, or did he kick and fight his father all the way to the altar? Where does a child's strength come from in moments like this?

As we left the office, I was stunned to see Dave running toward us.

"The lake patrol pulled me over." He came closer. "All they would say was there was a family emergency regarding my son, and they patched Ken through. He told me you would be here. Ken said it might be leukemia." Looking at Justin, he asked, "What's wrong?" He couldn't see it either.

How do I look my husband in the eyes and tell him his son has leukemia? I thought.

Justin, my innocent, little, brown-eyed boy, was looking up at me. In that moment, I did what had to be done. Dave's eyes filled with tears, and we hugged. Justin stood between us, clinging to our legs.

The doctor instructed us to go home and wait for the results. Once there, we became impatient. Our lives, the life of our precious firstborn, dangled before us like one of the characters from Justin's game, precarious, unsteady; but there was no button to push and no way to take control.

Jessica was home by then, smiling and dancing around her brother. Family and friends began to call.

"Pray that this is a mistake," we said again and again.

This filled the hours and kept our hearts hopeful that God would intervene. After all, I thought, *We are strong believers. We are good people. If it is leukemia, it could go away if God wills it to.* Back then, that's how my prayers were: ask and you shall receive, like I had a fairy godmother who could wave her silver wand and make bad things go away. Years of practicing prayer in less significant life situations made getting on my knees the natural thing to do. My prayers were automatic and silent.

Dave called Pastor Jim from our church. Like throwing a stone into a pond, prayers rippled outward.

This was the most helpless I had ever felt. It was the first time I understood real love. I would have slipped out of my skin and into Justin's if it meant sparing him.

We waited at home for a call from the oncology team at Childrens Hospital Los Angeles.

"Someone from their oncology team will call you," Dr. V had said.

But that night, no one called. *Pediatric oncology. Pediatric oncology.* The thought of needing them was beyond my grasp. *Dear God, what is happening?* I didn't know how to navigate this scene yet.

Justin ate dinner, played with Jessica, and crawled into our bed for the night. There, between Dave and me, his breathing was easy like when he was an infant. I slept with the phone at arm's reach. The next morning, there was still no phone call. We packed our bags not knowing what to bring or where to go when we got there. Ken stayed home with Jessica and fielded the phone.

We sat without looking at each other. If we did, we knew we'd fall apart. Dave drove along the I-5 South to Los Angeles, both of us lost in thought, too afraid to speak.

"Where are we going, Mommy?" Justin asked.

"We're going to see another doctor, big guy. Are you feeling okay?"

"Yes, Mommy," Justin replied, looking out the window as we left the cookie-cutter neighborhoods of Santa Clarita.

"It won't take too long, big guy," Dave said, trying to comfort.

I kept looking back at Justin, assessing him for signs or symptoms of distress. That's what nurses are taught to do. Holding his hand, still trying with my eyes to see the illness, how big it was, he looked no different today than he had yesterday.

All the while, I prayed, *Let this be some kind of mistake. When we arrive, please let someone say, "I'm sorry for the mix-up. These are not your son's lab results. Someone else's child has leukemia, not yours."*

Dave took the Los Feliz Boulevard exit. I stared out the window into the hectic, compressed atmosphere of Los Angeles. I noticed a few children already riding the miniature train that morning at the entrance to Griffith Park. They were smiling, healthy, carefree.

We pulled to the front of Childrens Hospital. I wondered about the apostrophe noticeably absent in the name. The large, circular driveway was not clogged. We parked in the passenger loading and unloading area where the golden arches of a McDonald's restaurant greeted us.

Justin smiled at the sight. "Can I get a Happy Meal, Mommy?"

He must have thought we were going to a mall, not a hospital. It seemed strange that a restaurant serving fast food was attached to a healthcare facility, but we were hungry, so I considered it.

"Let's go inside the hospital and get you checked in first. And then we can eat." Dave, quiet and sullen, agreed.

We didn't know how to do this, how to enter a world we wanted no part of, where to go, whom to talk to.

As I look back on it, winding up at Childrens Hospital with my own sick child was one of the cruelest ironies in my life. I'd been to Childrens once before as a newly minted nurse looking for work, but after a tour of the facility—ICU, ER, HEM ONC—I chose not to work there out of fear mostly. I took a less taxing job as a postpartum nurse at a small hospital close to home. I never thought I would use my nursing skills more for my own children than for others.

I liked working where new life began, where exhausted but exuberant mothers held their newborns to their breasts for the first time. I enjoyed caring for their babies, especially giving them their first bath, combing out the thick gunk, the dried blood and cheesy vernix from their silken hair, soaping them up with fresh-scented baby wash and rinsing away the trauma of birth. I'd wrap their slippery bodies in soft, warm blankets until they were just the right temperature and then pull their tightly wound arms through tiny white T-shirts, slipping their cone-shaped heads through an opening not too unlike the one they just exited. I'd wrap them like a burrito, hand them to their mothers, and wonder what the future held for them—whether joy or tragedy would sway their lives.

We passed the glass double doors of Childrens Hospital and made our way through admitting, where we signed papers and answered questions.

"What is the reason for your visit?" The woman on the other side of the desk wrote quick, blunt strokes and did not look up.

"Um, our son might have leukemia. We were told to bring him here," I said without looking away.

She picked up the phone. "No beds available yet? All right. I'll tell them to wait."

I couldn't believe it. This massive hospital was filled to capacity with children sicker than mine. In my mind, cancer trumped everything.

"Should we go to the emergency room?" I asked.

"No. We will call you when a room is ready," she said in a monotone voice.

Where does one wait knowing their child has leukemia? I thought. Where else?

McDonald's, of course. We ordered a Happy Meal, a Big Mac, and a Filet-O-Fish.

Somewhere between the French fries and the chicken nuggets, Justin made the decision that he liked "this doctor" better already.

When a bed became available, we took the giraffe elevator up to the fourth floor oncology wing. We entered, with a keen awareness of the indoor noise pollution, the *Bling! Bling-bling! Bling!* of the IV monitors, the ring of modern phones and the unfiltered chatter of housekeepers, ward clerks, lab techs and nurses.

Blood Brothers

Petite, pale patients gowned in blue pushed IV poles with dangling bags of blood infusing as they walked. Their bald heads confirmed that we were on the right floor. Someone greeted us and directed us to our room. It was Justin's room, but it was ours too. There was another bed in the room already occupied. The curtain was drawn, and we heard whispers and the familiar sound of *Sesame Street's sunny days… sweeping the clouds away…* coming from a television. We obeyed the directions to dress Justin in the hospital gown lying on the bed. What I really wanted to do was whisk him away. I was accustomed to adult and newborn patients—not children, not *my* child. Afraid, and awkward, a feeling of helplessness began to surface. The idea that the God I trusted may not make this go away was becoming reality.

A nurse entered our room with kind words and reassurances. She was younger than me.

"If you have to have cancer, this is the one to have. This is the good one," she said.

Dave and I sat on the bed, Justin between us; I felt like he was our pup and we were the two guard dogs. A few minutes passed. Vital signs were taken, and in a short time an IV was started in his hand. Blood was drawn and just like that, our son was a cancer kid.

Justin endured another bone marrow aspiration test, this time with the aid of anesthesia. When he awoke, he did not know that his parents had been standing in the corner of the room, holding each other, crying. He had no clue that Dave, his all-powerful Papa, as he called him, had to leave the room because the pain of watching his son's little body being pushed and pulled while a needle was pressed through bone almost brought him to his knees. It was better this way, Justin not knowing.

It was confirmed. Justin had acute lymphocytic leukemia, or ALL, and now joined the 2,500 other children diagnosed with leukemia in the U.S. each year. Dr. Judy Sato was assigned as Justin's oncologist. She was short in stature but tall in confidence. Her black, straight hair was cut in a blunt bob and framed her round face at the chin. Her white lab coat was clean and crisp. I studied her. I wondered what motivated her to practice this kind of medicine.

"Do you have children?" I asked.

"None of my own, but I think of my patients as my children," she said, placing her arm around Justin's shoulder. I liked her. Most mothers will put their kids before themselves, which meant she was likely to do the same.

Justin's blood was B-positive, like mine. I was only allowed to give him my blood once. When I donated for him, feeling the prick of the needle penetrate my skin, seeing the red of my blood fill the empty bag, made me feel connected to his fight. It comforted me to join him. I would have emptied myself if it would have saved his life. Donating gave me something important to do, an action to help him. It was better than sitting around, eating fast food. There would be many more days of waiting and worrying and eating poorly.

When cancer began twenty-four hours earlier, Justin had been sitting on our living room floor, a child at play. He'd learned a secret way to earn more lives by trapping a little turtle, and he couldn't wait to get it in exactly the right position at the base of what looked like a staggered block staircase. When my eyes had welled with tears at hearing the word leukemia through the phone, his eyes had remained fixed on the television screen.

As my mind was being shoved into the world of childhood leukemia, he had stood up straight and tall and cried out suddenly, "Look, Mommy! I trapped the turtle!" A bright green turtle bounced back and forth on the screen like a ping-pong ball. The jackpot sound of a slot machine chimed as the number increased. When it stopped, he turned to me, his eyes wide with excitement and said, "Now I have a hundred lives."

The Other Side of Mother Nurse

I had finally fallen asleep when I heard the door crack. It was late, and I couldn't see the clock. I was tired and teary. In a hospital, time, unlike intake and output, goes unmeasured. That first night at Childrens Hospital, lying on a cot three feet from Justin, I'd felt too far away; so I had gotten up and squeezed into his narrow bed. His soft skin and warm feet quelled the cold, unfamiliar feel of his semi-private room. We had been alone in the "A" bed, closest to the bathroom. The room was small and cramped. There was a long window at shoulder level next to the door that let in light and peering eyes. I had pulled the shade down earlier, but even so, I felt like a mouse in a cage. The only thing missing was the hamster wheel.

The hum of the IV monitor muffled the outside noises, but not enough. I'd closed the pale, striped curtain that hung from the ceiling to shroud Justin's bed. As a nurse, I'd done this for strangers a thousand times, but the fabric barrier was no match for the voices of late-night passersby. Their hushed tones took me back to a time when I was the nurse on the other side.

A teenage boy was brought in on a gurney. I heard one nurse whisper to the other, "He fractured his leg. Osteosarcoma."

Bone cancer, I thought. Sometimes, being a nurse, I knew things. When it came to lying in bed with my own son's cancer, I knew too little.

As Justin slept and the young man moaned, the night's interruptions dominated my attempts at sleep. I listened to the young man's mother pray in Spanish. She wept. I thought I heard rosary beads tapping. I didn't fully understand her language, but I knew her despair.

Somewhere between diagnosis and treatments, the gurney came for Justin. He would have surgery to place a central intravenous line into a large blood vessel above his heart, called a Hickman catheter. Its double lumens would be used to infuse blood and medications as well as withdraw blood for lab tests. Chemotherapy would be given through this line, chemicals too toxic for vulnerable peripheral veins.

Dave and I handed our sleepy boy over to strangers. They took him behind closed doors, and I quickly learned the importance of trusting our medical team, but trust does not come overnight, if it comes at all. I checked identification badges, IV bag labels, and name bracelets, anything I could to assure that things were being done right. I'd been imagining every worst-case scenario when a nurse in blue scrubs entered the waiting room.

"Would you like to see Justin?"

Dave and I jumped to our feet, almost knocking over the cold remains of coffee.

"Not many parents get to come into recovery this soon," she said, holding the door open for us. "Sometimes children come out of anesthesia like wild cats, crying and fighting. They pull at their tubes. You can imagine how scary that would be, but your son is so calm."

Blood Brothers

This did not surprise me. Justin was born that way. He practically delivered himself. When my body opened to release him and the obstetrician cried, "Don't push," Justin's head descended into his hands.

"Phew. You're just in time," the delivery nurse had commented.

Justin, just in time, he lived up to his name. In the quiet hours after the celebrating and stitching, when I held him in my arms, alone, I felt the warmth of his breath against my face. In the midst of that most blissful moment, I had the overwhelming sense of the deepest sorrow. I knew that something tragic was going to happen to him. Astonished and confused by this understanding, I dismissed the experience as hormones and never mentioned it to anyone. But I had never forgotten that moment; and now, walking into recovery with its rows of small gurneys and seeing him lying so still, I knew hormones weren't to blame.

I recognized Justin immediately, and we rushed to his side. He was sleeping, his chest rising and falling as though he were at home, asleep, in his own bed. Dave and I took turns kissing him. We touched his arms and rubbed his feet. He opened his eyes, grinned, and closed them again. Even under medications, he was docile.

I lifted his gown to see the catheter. Protruding through his once-pristine skin was a thick, white tube about eight inches long. It was bigger than I had expected. The end had two separate white, plastic caps dangling from the main stem, which almost reached his belly button. Blood about the size of a dime stained the dressing higher up.

The Hickman would be there for at least a year.

It meant fewer needle sticks, less pain, better drug absorption, and easy access. But it would be my responsibility to clean it, change the caps, and flush it daily to prevent clots. I was not familiar with it. I had never taken care of any central line. Now I would be going home with one hanging from my son's chest, vulnerable to all things childlike: bacteria, moisture, and trauma.

"Good thing your mommy is a nurse."

I'd heard this over and over again since entering the hospital, but I had trouble shaking the "you nurses" comment from Dr. V. There was so much that I didn't understand about this disease. I did not trust myself.

A couple of days later, we were introduced to another roommate—a precocious four-year-old girl named Blare.

"Are they ready to draw my labs yet?" she asked the nurse in a tone that revealed her seasoned veteran status. She had neuroblastoma, a cancer I'd never heard of, one of many. She had been diagnosed two years prior. It was comforting to meet parents who had survived the first days of diagnosis and lived to tell about it.

"She doesn't have the good cancer, like Justin," I said to Dave later.

I'm ashamed to say that knowing someone had it worse than we did bolstered me as we faced day after day of adjusting to hospital life.

One way to cope was to walk. One day Justin and I stepped outside to the front garden. I pushed his IV pole with one hand and held his hand with the other. The fresh air felt good. When I returned, Dave was trembling. A family member of mine had stopped in for a visit. He found Dave alone and proceeded to tell him that the reason Justin was sick was because we were too "busy." In his opinion we needed to slow the pace of our lives and "rest." In other words, Justin's leukemia was our fault. He believed it was his duty to say what was wrong with us. I had already felt intense guilt. It was an automatic response. We'd gone down the list of possible causes—the water (we should have bought filtered), the air (we should have purified it), the house (we should have checked for asbestos). Thankfully our medical team was not as ignorant as my relative. They reassured us that it was common for parents to go through a period of guilt and feel responsible for their child's cancer, and they informed us that Justin's cancer was not caused by anything we could have prevented.

Two weeks after admission, we were discharged. I was surprised by this. All of the treatments for the rest of the year would be done on an outpatient basis. Returning home was an event. The carpets had been cleaned, our dog cast outside, and a note placed on the door: "Do not enter if you are sick." Even with all the changes, coming home felt like we had exited on to the sunny side of a long, dark tunnel.

Justin and I returned to the outpatient clinic practically every day for chemo, blood transfusions, platelets, spinal taps, exams, and radiation. By day twenty-eight he was in remission, which was a good thing considering he had been placed in the high-risk category at diagnosis. The earlier remission is obtained the better. Sometimes I took Jessica with us, but she was a bit unruly, as most two-year-olds are, so family and friends became her daily babysitters. Uncle Ken lived with us, and he helped when he wasn't working. He hired a housekeeper to clean every other week. Meals from church members and parents from Dave's cross-country team came on a regular basis. Keeping Justin alive was a community effort.

As we adjusted to our new lives, Dave's commitment to his runners never diminished. Being the supportive wife, I had attended most of the team's races with Justin and Jessica. With leukemia in the family, I found myself less able to keep up, and it started to seem like I shouldn't have to. As my focus on Justin's care increased, so did Dave's intensity for his athletes. I had taken a leave of absence from the hospital I'd been working for and committed myself to caring for Justin and Jessica first and foremost. I was too naïve to know that I needed Dave's help more now than ever. I didn't see his retreat to his team as the problem it was.

Justin endured many kinds of treatments, but cranial radiation was the strangest. You couldn't see it, taste it, or smell it. Blue dashes and dots on Justin's forehead, behind his ears, and at the base of his skull marked its location. Justin, ever cooperative, would lie down on the cold, metal table as though he were lying on our living room couch. A machine hovered over him, making humming noises. While most children try to leap from the table, he remained peaceful. He made treatments easy on me.

We saw Blare in the radiology department from time to time. Week by week, she withered away. Her lit face became a blank stare. Her limbs became thin and flaccid.

The radiology waiting room had proven to be an interesting place for Justin as he stared at the large, rectangular fish tank upon each visit. It was like a scene from the movie *Finding Nemo*. There were clown fish and angelfish, but one fish caught his attention.

"Mommy, look." He pointed through the glass. A gold fish with huge, bulging eyes and long, feathery fins swam gracefully among the others.

"How beautiful, big guy. That one is really pretty."

"No, Mommy. Look. It only has one eye." He pointed.

The fish turned and swam straight toward us, revealing that it, indeed, had only one eye.

"Take it out, Mommy. Take it out. We have to tell someone so they can take it out of the tank."

Justin's response to the fish's disfigurement took me by surprise. "Why? Big guy—"

"Because it is different. It can't stay in there."

"But look at him," I said. "He looks happy. He is swimming with all the others. And look. He is eating with all the others."

The fish nibbled.

"Yeah, but he looks weird without his eye," Justin pointed out.

"Maybe, but wouldn't it be better just to leave him alone? We don't have to *do* anything," I explained.

After some persuasion, Justin agreed, and every time we entered that waiting room—as his hair thinned and his cheeks bulged—he would run to the fish tank and look for the one-eyed goldfish. He was beginning to understand what it felt like to be the one who looked different.

I hated subjecting him to radiation. After all, this was Justin's brain here.

One month later, I noticed Justin smiling less. I had been told to expect depression as a side effect from the radiation and remembered little Blare. It was unnerving to see him staring into nowhere, distant. I had no one to compare Justin's reactions with except a child with a poorer prognosis.

Would his smile return? Where did my little boy go?

Four dim weeks later, our Justin began to return. To see him smile again gave us hope that he had recovered from radiation, as other bizarre side effects from chemo manifested. His cheeks became puffed up, and his eyes seemed to shrink.

I knew he would lose his hair but had not expected it to come out the way it did. One night, three months into treatment, I was giving Justin a bath. He was playing with his Ninja Turtle figurines in the tub. The Hickman catheter dangled from his bare skin above the water line. I knelt down and poured shampoo into the palm of my hand, massaged it into his hair, and noticed that it felt rough, like sand. His hair stuck to my skin. It started by the handful, and by the time I finished rinsing, he was bald. I could have cried but didn't want to upset him. Hair floated around him like debris after a shipwreck. He didn't like seeing his hair in the water instead of on his head, and he grabbed at the floating clumps in an attempt to put them back.

"Come on, big guy. Let's get you out of here."

As I lifted him out, hair stuck to his legs and feet. I wrapped him in a towel and cuddled with him on the bedroom floor as he stared at his bald head in the closet mirror. Touching his scalp, he cried. I cried. How to navigate hair loss with a five-year-old was not taught in Nursing 101. I'd learned proper hand washing, how to miter a mean bed corner, and even how to feel a newborn's pulse, but touching Justin's bare scalp was like nothing I had ever experienced. There was no peach fuzz. It was smooth like an apple with ten single strands of hair still clinging for dear life.

I considered covering all the mirrors in the house but decided against it. We had to get used to this disease and all it entailed. It took a few weeks before Justin became accustomed to seeing his round, smooth dome speckled with stray hairs. He looked rather birdlike. Justin had been bald as a baby. People loved to rub his perfect, bowling-ball-shaped head. Back then it was an endearing gesture. But now he was our five-year-old big guy, and he felt more comfortable if he wore a hat. He started to collect them: baseball, ski, sailor caps. My favorite was a sporty, neon orange and black cap with a short bill and a thick Velcro strap. I liked the way it framed his face and hugged the soft, bare curve of the back of his head. In the absence of eyebrows, a hat gave his face a place to stop.

Even though he covered his head when we went out, there were times when children made fun of him, public places like play grounds or grocery stores where kids pointed and stared. This was an adjustment, because Justin had always been beautiful, not only to me, but to most who saw him.

"What beautiful eyes," they'd comment as his thick, dark lashes waved up and down. Without lashes, his dark-brown eyes seemed black and deep and infinite.

Feeling like a freak show was new to us. I didn't like the fact that my good-looking son was on the receiving end of stares and pointed fingers. These were the days before *cancer* became a household word and hairlessness its synonym.

We stopped going to public places because of the risk of infection. On the dark days, when Justin was throwing up or feeling tired or bored, little sister Jessica would entertain us. She kept us on our toes. She would fall off of her chair or roll on the floor and then cuddle up to JD (his nickname). She kept him company while watching *Sesame Street* or *Barney*. Justin preferred Cookie Monster shoving crumbs into his furry face to the sweet, sappy singing of overzealous children. Jessica did whatever JD did. She wanted to be just like her big brother. When I changed the dressing on his Hickman catheter, she'd lay down next to him, lift up her T-shirt, and ask me to put tape on her chest too. "Like JD," she'd say. Even though it hurt to take it off, she wanted to be taped. She thought it was normal.

Life on treatment caused many new normals. Justin's appetite was one of them. It became ferocious. It was not unusual for him to wake up at three a.m. asking for pizza. "Now, please." We were told the medication, Prednisone, would do that. It also made his face and belly swollen and round. It could have made him irritable too, but we never saw this side effect. It was the crazy appetite that kept me busy. Once, at a restaurant, Justin ate half of an entire barbecued chicken, much to the dismay of the waitress who had bet him five dollars that he couldn't do it. He wiped barbeque sauce from his grinning face, patted his swollen belly, and collected the cash.

Treatments continued three months, six months, nine months, and then a year. Weeks and months of explaining treatment plans and lab values to family and friends had been exhausting and time consuming, but I was the nurse, so I did the researching and the explaining. There was no Internet, no Google, no text messaging.

Staying coupled with Dave was sometimes like chasing a wild pony. He didn't seem to understand that spending time at home had become a necessity. He would teach algebra classes all day, work out with the team every afternoon, come home to eat, and then correct homework papers while watching TV or talk on the phone with other coaches or news reporters interested in his team. On weekends he'd be gone coaching. The strange thing was that I was so consumed with caring for the kids that I didn't feel annoyed by his absence. We did things the old-fashioned way: Dave brought home the bacon, and I cooked it up in an overheating pan.

Receiving letters in the mail helped lift my spirits. I read them when I was alone—kind, uplifting words on paper from faraway places. I'd read them and sometimes cry. This way no one had to see my tears and I could react without feeling self conscious. It seemed to me that each time we needed money, a card would arrive with a gift inside. When people ask me now, "What can I do?" if someone they know has been diagnosed. "Send a note," is my response. "Include a gift card." Not earning an income anymore had been taking its toll. Our gas expense had tripled, parking fees and medical co-payments were added expenses our budget did not have room for. I missed earning an income and didn't like relying on Dave for money, even though he was never one to belittle me or even question where his paycheck went. It was a matter of pride to be able to help pay the bills. I managed our finances and liked the feeling of independence I had in doing so; but with the added stressors, Dave's lack of interest in financial matters was frustrating at times. Receiving a card with a monetary gift was always a welcome sight, and if we didn't need it I could easily give it to someone else who did.

But the mail brought news too, the kind that was difficult to receive. Little Blare, Justin's former roommate, had passed away. The invitation to her funeral left my heart aching for her family. "Such nice people," I'd said. "So undeserving. Such a lovely child."

This won't happen to us. Our son has the "good" cancer.

This I had to believe. We didn't tell Justin about Blare.

Justin survived the trauma of the first year of chemotherapy, radiation, spinal taps, bone marrow aspirations, and doctor visits while maintaining remission. He had dodged leukemia and was only hospitalized twice: two weeks at diagnosis and two nights for a fever of unknown origin. Almost a year after having the central IV inserted, it was removed, leaving behind a small scar that looked a bit like the bullet wounds I'd seen in nursing school.

Maintain

The maintenance phase of therapy meant daily oral chemo: 6 MP, Prednisone, and Methotrexate, and monthly Vincristine by IV, which was started in his hand and then removed the same day. Justin still had to have a lumbar puncture every three months to examine his spinal fluid and inject chemo. He had a bone marrow aspiration every six months to look for hidden leukemia cells. The lumbar punctures were still done with only a topical anesthesia. Justin was so cooperative about this procedure, even though it hurt, that the medical team filmed him having it done to use as a teaching tool to prepare other children.

The maintenance regimen was much easier and caused less obvious side effects. Justin's hair grew back. His puffy cheeks diminished, and he smiled often. One would never know that this little boy was on chemotherapy. Justin and I became fans of playing Tetris on matching Game Boys in the waiting room on clinic days. I would laugh as we stacked little blocks on the game's screen and sent them to each other's game, forcing the opponent to lose. He'd scream, and then, in a little while, he'd send them back to me and I'd scream. The hours spent playing seemed like minutes. Sometimes we'd stop for dinner at Chin Chin in Studio City. Nurse Kathy had recommended it one day at clinic. We'd sit at the counter and watch the noodles and bell peppers be tossed from wok to wok by skilled chefs wearing white hats.

If Justin had a painful procedure, like a lumbar puncture or bone marrow aspiration, I'd take him to the toy store.

"Pick one toy that costs no more than ten dollars," I'd say, and he would smile.

It was not unusual for Justin to still be trying to decide an hour later. One time, he left with only a small rubber ball.

Bringing homemade cookies to clinic put a smile on Justin's face. Making clinic visits more pleasant for him put a smile on mine. It was a simple trick I'd learned to make the experience more palatable.

Starting kindergarten at age six did not pose any of the typical, "Mommy, don't leave me," challenges. Justin was small for his age, but with a five-foot-tall mother, it was possible his size was more a product of genetics than chemotherapy and radiation. He never cried for me to stay. On the first day of school, wearing his blue jeans and a plaid, button-up shirt, his hair combed neatly to one side, he waved from over his shoulder and never looked back.

I wrote a letter to the other parents in the class, disclosing to them that my son had been treated for leukemia and it was imperative that I be informed if their child had any contagious diseases like chicken pox. Most of the parents were supportive and understood the importance of early detection for kids with compromised immune systems, but one woman called and wanted to know if she should pull her child out of the class because she didn't want her son to catch leukemia too. I expected most people to have a basic working knowledge about leukemia, the most common of all childhood cancers, since I knew it intimately. She wanted to know why Justin still needed to be on chemo if the leukemia was gone. The way it was explained to me by Dr. Sato was the way I explained it to her.

"Remission doesn't necessarily mean that all of the cancer cells are gone, simply that they cannot be found. Think of cancer cells as Rambos hiding in a jungle. They are very good at concealing themselves so they keep giving chemo even after the disease stage is over, in case one of them pops up without us seeing it. It is a precaution taken even though the cancer may already be gone forever."

I reassured the classmate's mother that according to lab results, not only were no leukemia cells seen, but even if leukemia cells appeared, they would not be contagious. I learned to discuss Justin's illness more discretely and to provide correct information to those who needed it. I didn't like being the poster mother for childhood cancer. I wanted normalcy again.

I returned to working the evening shift twice a week. Uncle Ken moved out. Dave was busy teaching and coaching. Justin was doing well in school and was happy to be there. He rarely missed a day and caught few colds. I kept him home from time to time if he seemed overly tired or if I knew a particular illness was going around.

Kindergarten came and went, as did first and second grade, without a hitch. Justin played t-ball one year and then baseball after that. Dave started becoming more engaged with him, as they both liked playing catch. Jessica enjoyed sliding down the dirt hill at his games. He felt good, looked healthy, and had a full life with friends, re-enacting *Teenage Mutant Ninja Turtles* and playing video games.

Compared to the heavy-duty side effects from the first year of treatment, the slightly dark circles under Justin's eyes were the only visible side effect of maintenance therapy. I didn't mind the daily pill regimen; it made me feel like we were doing something to keep the leukemia at bay.

Newborn worries trumped old ones when baby number three was born. Justin, at age eight, enjoyed having another little sister: Joelle Marie. Jessica, four years old, welcomed the new baby too. Life was full, and Justin's visits to the oncology clinic were still limited to once a month. While having Joelle was a joyful time, it was also stressful.

Dave was running triathlons and biathlons and marathons as well as coaching and playing basketball and softball. Baby number three meant a repeat of the distancing Dave had done when Justin was sick. This time I felt lonely and abandoned when he was out running and came home too exhausted to help. It was as though the hidden frustrations I'd had with Dave while Justin was sick began to surface.

It was an adjustment for all of us to have a new baby around. Justin took well to it. We discovered that he loved babies and babies loved him. I had never known a boy his age to stop playing a video game just to hold his baby sister, but he did that over and over again.

When the maintenance phase of treatment ended, three years after its inception, a part of me didn't want to let it go. It felt like I was leaving my son unarmed in a war zone. We had four years of one kind of chemo or another, steroids, antibiotics, all kinds of pills every day. And then, one day, it was all over. No more pills. We just walked out the clinic doors and waved to the pharmacist on our way out. When you have the power of the pill clutched in the palm of your hand, and the feeling of helplessness rises, you have to peel away one finger at a time.

There were days when I wanted to bring Justin back to the clinic before his scheduled appointments. I needed to know his blood counts were okay. We had been told that if he was going to relapse, it was more likely to happen in the first year off maintenance. I'd learned a thing or two about relapses in the hours and hours of hanging out in the waiting room with other cancer families. I could tell just by looking at them. One month, they were all smiles and their child had a head full of hair; and then a few months later, they were sullen, and their child was wearing a hat.

As time passed, it became easier to let go of the fear of relapse. Juggling three kids, a husband with athletic ambitions beyond his fatherly time constraints, work, church, and family placed leukemia a little further down the list of things to worry about.

Blood Brothers

I was discovering the busyness that came with a healthy family and the stress that accompanied ten years of marriage. Financial needs, three children, work stresses; like all human beings on planet earth, we had our share of trouble. Too many trouble-filled days in a row wore me down at times. There were seasons when everything seemed to be falling apart: one week the refrigerator leaked, ruining the wood floors; and the swamp cooler broke in hundred-degree heat, leaving us all sweating and thirsty. And after getting that fixed, black toilet water started backing up into our shower. Looking skyward, waving my rubber-gloved fists, I remember saying out loud, "Isn't having a kid with cancer enough? Do I have to put up with this crap too?"

Over time, having had a sick child, my life perspective changed. When a friend of mine told me that her teenage daughter was pregnant, she was obviously upset. I knew she thought I should be too, but I wasn't. I wondered if Justin would be able to father a child someday. Sometimes, when I saw parents badgering their kids over a missed shot in a basketball game or a slower-than-expected race time or putting them down for the frumpy clothes they had on or freaking out over the milk they'd spilt, I just wanted to shake them and say, "Be glad they're here to spill that milk."

I was beginning to see that Dave's way of dealing with Justin's illness had been to stay busy and focus on his team and his training. Mine was to pick up the slack and focus on each child, trying to keep everybody happy.

Now and then, I wondered what life without leukemia would look like—an easy life with an outgoing husband three active children free from the shadow cast by a life-threatening illness. Days like that came, and just as I began to relax, another crisis would come along, like the head-on collision Dave and Jessica were in. They could have died in an instant as they traveled home from the beach with the team and the van rolled three times before it rested on its side. Jessica was five years old. She remembered the sound of screams, the broken glass, and the blood pouring over Dave's face.

She and eight other kids were with him in our van. Miraculously, no one was killed. Jessica was bruised, and Dave received stitches on his scalp where his head had grazed the asphalt. I called the ER and the nurse told me Jessica was okay, that Dave was getting X-rays and would call me. At first, I felt relief, then anger.

"What did you do?" I asked Dave. "Is Jessica okay?"

"Yeah." His voice shook. "It wasn't my fault."

They suffered minor injuries that day. No one was seriously hurt, not even the driver who had fallen asleep at the wheel and caused the accident. But my accusatory attitude was a symptom of a hurting marriage. Had I forgotten all that we had been through with Justin? With each other? After cancer, there was a sort of calm that gave rise to inner grumblings which needed to be addressed. Eventually, after counseling and many long walks, they were brought to the surface where Dave and I worked hard to tackle the problems. We didn't want a marriage that looked happy on the outside but was filled with hate on the inside. Our kids were watching us navigate life as much as we were watching them.

As the years went by, Justin's appearance began to change. His jaw seemed squarer, his eyebrows became thicker, and a small dimple began to emerge on his chin, like my dad, his grandpa, Richie. His eyes sparkled, and his voice cracked when he least expected it—a sure sign of his entering manhood. He loved running and weight lifting, and his lean, muscular body showed it. He was proud of being "buff," as the kids called it, and enjoyed flexing like Hulk Hogan for us. He was small in stature but tall in charisma. He was what the girls at his school called a hottie. I know this because I heard them once when I was picking him up from school.

Justin and Jessica had both qualified for the junior Olympics in cross-country that year, which was held in Knoxville, Tennessee. At the start of his race, a flurry of feet of over two hundred kids fought for position. I couldn't even find Justin among the stampede. But then I spotted him—his balanced stride, like a fingerprint, unique to him. Most of the kids he raced against towered over him by a foot or more. He ran all out and stayed in the middle of the pack.

While other parents shouted, "Faster, faster!" or "What's the matter with you, Johnny? Come on!" I ran to every visible sighting spot and shouted, "Go, Justin. You're doing great. Nice job." When he crossed that finish line in a hundred and sixtieth place, I cried.

There are all kinds of tragedies. For Justin to have survived cancer and then had his parents succumb to the pressures of divorce was one we were able to avoid. The best way to manage our marriage in the midst of illness was to find a better way to balance Dave's recreation with mine. Swing dancing was becoming popular at the time, so I talked Dave into taking a class through our city's parks and rec program. It quickly became evident that my loving husband's ability to keep time with the quick-footed steps was not his forte. It was his willingness to try that made me feel loved.

One night Dave could not attend class, so Justin, then fourteen, offered to sub. "I'll go with you, Mom." Not many boys his age were hot on the idea of taking swing dance classes with their mothers, but this was my Justin—charming, optimistic, and adventurous. He took to swing dancing with ease. He had clean lines and a polished look from the start. My boy had rhythm, and I didn't ask Dave back. Justin and I spent the few remaining classes enjoying the triple step, rock step danced to saxophones, trumpets, and trombones from Big Band icons Benny Goodman and Glenn Miller.

Justin was happiest when we were together as a family. His smile was brightest when he was wrestling on the floor, Joelle on his back and Jessica pinned underneath him. As the rubble from one crisis or another settled, I felt a sense of accomplishment that our family had survived intact. We attended our neighborhood church together. We ate our meals together. We took modest vacations together. It was as if a dark curtain had been lifted and the light of day filtered throughout our home.

Lisa Solis DeLong

Shoes On the Crosswalk

It was a Monday morning in February 1999 when the phone rang. I expected it to be a friend calling about the kids coming over after school. Dave, ready to leave for work, answered in the kitchen. Joelle, in first grade, and Jessica, in fifth, grabbed their backpacks and headed for the door, ready to walk the half block to school. Justin, still not feeling well, had come downstairs and crawled into our bed with baby Jacob.

The kids had been ill all week. For the young ones, the slight cough, low-grade fever, and body aches went away quickly, but Justin's lingered. The lymph nodes along his jaw line became swollen. I'd suspected mumps and took him to the pediatrician to get his blood drawn on Friday. As I came into the living room expecting to help get the girls out the door, the tardy bell rang in the distance. Dave hung up the phone, his face blank, staring.

"That was the pediatrician," he said, lowering his gaze. "He has Justin's lab results. The leukemia, it's back."

I walked over to the couch and sat down.

I could hear Jacob cooing as Justin talked to him. "D'ya like that, little guy. Huh?"

I felt what I imagine my friend Lois must have felt when she was hit by a truck while crossing the street, the impact so great that her shoes were still in the crosswalk, her body a hundred feet away. After being in remission for almost ten years, the cancer was back in my athletic, handsome, teenage boy. I sat on the couch, rocked back and forth, covered my face, and cried.

"No, no, no! It can't be back!"

Dave swept the girls out the door. Their questioning, brown eyes looked back at me. I was unable to speak. He sent them off to school, walked toward the couch, and began to pace back and forth, biting his nails. I wanted to yell for the girls to come back but couldn't find the words.

"They think he's relapsed. His white cell count is over a hundred and ninety thousand. Dr. Kim wants us to get to City of Hope as soon as possible."

As soon as possible, when it comes to leukemia, is immediately. That's how cancer is. One moment you are planning mashed potatoes and gravy for dinner, and then, with one ring of the phone, you're planning trips to the oncology ward.

Please, God, please let this be a mistake, I prayed.

We sat on the couch for a moment. Dave looked at me.

"We have to tell Justin."

I was crying too hard.

Dave said, "We'll tell him together. I'll go to work, let my students into the classroom, and get another teacher to cover for me. I'll be right back."

His work was only a couple of blocks away, so I agreed.

I sat on the couch and wrapped my arms around myself. "How could you, Lord? He's been through enough," I mumbled. "He doesn't deserve this! Why my sweet Justin? Why now?"

Justin called from the bedroom, "Mom, come change this stinky little guy."

I used to have the ability to stay composed in a crisis, but not this time. I knew I couldn't walk in that bedroom without falling apart, so I cleared my throat and yelled back, "I'll be there in a minute." I had to get a grip. Holding my head in my hands, I prayed, "Lord, this is too much. Please help me to be the kind of mom Justin needs to get through this. Please give me courage." I held Justin off as long as I could. I started to make my way to the bedroom when Dave returned. Our pastor was with him. Pastor Jim Ryan, originally from Texas, was a big man with a heart to match. With his warm Southern drawl, he'd welcomed us into Heart of the Canyons church years ago. He lived a block away from us, and I was glad he had come. His hug was as comforting as his ability to pray for us. Dave had seen Jim driving up the street on the way back from the high school and waved him down.

We stood in the living room.

"I'm his father," Dave said. "I want to be the one to tell him."

While Jim stayed in the living room and prayed, Dave and I went into the bedroom. Justin was lying on his side, his head resting on his hand, tickling Jacob's feet. He smiled and looked like a kid with a mild case of the flu. I studied him more closely, looking for signs indicating the seriousness of his illness, but there were none, no bruises, no bleeding gums, and no complaints of bone pain. The same feeling of inadequacy at identifying his illness was there in me again. Only this time, I was not naïve to the perils of treatment that lay ahead.

It had been almost ten years since Justin's original diagnosis. The idea that the leukemia could come back had been a powerful one when he was six; but as each year had passed, it faded. We did not socialize with other families within a pediatric cancer support group, nor did we attend holiday parties or events affiliated with oncology centers. We were too busy living. I would not say that we pretended Justin's leukemia was gone or that we were being ostriches. In those days we believed it was gone because we became accustomed to wellness and assumed good health would remain. By the time Justin was thirteen, he had a couple of vague memories of hospital stays when he was little. Now, at fourteen, he knew health more than sickness, and in his mind leukemia was a thing of the past.

"What took you so long? This little guy is getting fussy." His voice cracked.

I picked up Jacob and sat close to Justin.

"Big guy, I'm really sorry to have to tell you this," Dave began. He sat on the bed and put his hand on Justin's leg. Clearing his throat, he continued. "That was the doctor on the phone. He thinks your leukemia is back."

Justin, holding Jacob's hand, looked down in silence.

"Does this mean I can't go to school anymore? How can it be back? It's been so long? Can I still run track?"

I couldn't remember the last time I'd seen him cry, but tears began to flow. I tried to hide the fear in my eyes, but I don't think I did a very good job. In moments like this, your whole body weeps. We held each other and tried to encourage Justin. Pastor Jim offered to pick up the girls from school, and we began the practical task of saving Justin's life again. Dave picked up the baby, Justin went upstairs to get dressed, and I called the outpatient pediatric oncology clinic at City of Hope.

"We're coming in," I said.

From the first time we pulled into the parking lot at City of Hope, we felt taken care of, partly because we didn't have to fight for a place to park and we didn't have to pay. Most major medical centers require that you pay anywhere from seven to sixteen dollars to park no matter how sick the child. Your kid might have died at their facility that day, but you still have to pay to leave. This enrages me, especially when I am fumbling through my purse at the parking lot ticket booth looking for the money I forgot to bring or that I had to spend unexpectedly inside the facility that day.

City of Hope was a longer drive for us, but it was slower paced, tranquil. The beautiful rose gardens and expansive green lawns were a stark contrast to the concrete jungle that was Childrens Hospital Los Angeles, where Justin was originally diagnosed and treated nearly ten years prior. Even though he had received excellent care at CHLA, and we loved the team of experts there when he was little, it felt right to be at City of Hope now that Justin was in his teens.

Three years prior, while Justin was on maintenance, we had followed Justin's oncologist, Dr. Sato, to City of Hope after she left CHLA. The biannual checkups at City of Hope, which we had become accustomed to, had been pleasant ones. Being that Justin was a busy teenager, the forty-five-mile drive to Duarte afforded me the chance to have him all to myself. He'd tell me something about how he liked playing football in the school Turkey Bowl, and then I'd tease him about how big his muscles were getting. It was always easy to be in Justin's company.

When Justin was thirteen, we threw him a big birthday party to celebrate being in remission for five years past chemotherapy treatments. He was considered clinically cured.

We told his oncologist about the celebration, and she said, "That's great, but I've still seen kids relapse this far out. I still want to see you every six months."

While that wasn't exactly the response I'd wanted, I had to admit that's what I liked about her. She was honest and up front. When your child is ill, you look at their doctor for clues, all the time wondering if they are keeping something from you. *Was that a raised eyebrow? Do they know my child's cancer is impossible to beat? That hand combing through their hair, are they appeasing me with answers to ease the pain?* I'd known Dr. Sato long enough to know how to read her. She was at the forefront of the battle against childhood cancers and had devoted her life to trying to save children afflicted with the disease. I respected her and admired her intelligence and her commitment. I trusted her experience and her intuition. Though Justin had so many years of wellness, it was important to me to maintain that rapport with Justin's oncologist just in case we needed her down the road.

We drove to City of Hope with the same kind of numb silence as we had in 1990. We parked and walked past the bronze sculpture of a mother and father holding a child upward as they appeared to float above water, past the row of wheelchairs parked like taxi cabs waiting for a passenger, through the glass double doors. Justin was strong enough to walk on his own, but Dave and I had him flanked on either side just in case. We didn't say much along the way. Even though we had been through these doors before, it felt strange, scary.

For three years, we had been arriving at City of Hope with a survivor, sitting in the waiting room, watching the patients with no hair and swollen faces come and go. At that time, I could have worn a T-shirt with "My child survived cancer" printed on it or placed one of those "Proud Parent of an Honor Student at City of Hope" bumper stickers on my forehead. It felt so good for Justin to be a survivor.

I'd asked Justin once if he remembered the bone marrow aspirations he'd endured when he was little, where they would bore a needle through his pelvic bone and pull vigorously on the syringe to withdraw bone marrow. He shrugged his shoulders.

"No. Not really."

I was thankful for that, especially because in those days, these procedures were done without anesthesia, and he whimpered while I held him down, tears running down our cheeks. I shuddered at the thought of having to endure so much suffering again.

We had to let the reality of Justin being one of them—a cancer patient—soak in. The pale faces, sunken eyes, bald heads, blank canvasses being repainted one microscopic cell at a time, looking at us in the waiting room, served as poignant reminders of what lay ahead. Handsome Justin, his hair sculpted into a meticulous flattop, sat between Dave and me, immersed in dread.

The clinic was calm and quiet. The clerks, nurses, and attendants smiled kindly. Our wait was short. We met with Dr. Sato, who, in her usual straightforward way, primed us for what lay ahead. She spoke directly to Justin, which I liked and so did he.

She said, "Justin, this relapse means there is going to be a battle and you are going to have to fight very hard to beat this cancer. I'm going to do everything I can to help you 'cause I'm a fighter, but I need you to be a fighter too. Will you fight this, Justin? Are you a fighter?"

Justin smiled, nodded his head, looked down at the floor and then at her, and said, "Yeah. I'm a fighter."

Right then, I recalled a moment when Justin was little, maybe four years old, where he was anything but a fighter. We were sitting in a waiting room to have his picture taken. He was playing with a Mr. Potato Head toy when a younger child, probably three years old, came up to him and grabbed Mr. Potato Head out of his hands. Even though Justin was bigger, he just let it go, didn't fight back, and didn't even complain. This was my Justin, the most gentle person I have ever known, and under the circumstances this troubled me. I knew his spirit. I had carried it within me; and though I never said it, I wasn't sure he was mean enough to beat this cancer.

She said, "We have to do a bone marrow aspiration test to find out if the same leukemia has returned or if it has changed."

Very often, a relapse involves an entirely different cancer because the treatments themselves are carcinogens.

"Please tell me advancements in anesthesia have been made since our last experience," I asked.

"Oh yes," Dr. Sato explained. "Justin will be under a kind of twilight anesthesia right here on our outpatient unit. He won't remember a thing."

We were introduced to a pediatric intencivist, Dr. Arcenue, a pleasant Filipino man whose skills included administering anesthesia here in the clinic. Even though I was a nurse, I did not know all that his title meant, so I asked.

"I take care of the very critical, very sick kids. You don't ever want to need me," he said with a light-hearted smile.

He joked around with Justin and put him at ease. We were relieved not only that there would be little or no pain for Justin but also to be in the hands of someone who made Justin laugh, seemed happy to be there, and was super skilled and confident.

An intravenous line was started in Justin's arm, blood was drawn, and the bone marrow aspiration was done. Unlike when Justin was five, I didn't feel the need to stay and hold him; and he neither did he. Dave and I waited outside the procedure room. When Justin woke up after the procedure, he had no memory of it as promised. This is where trust is nurtured, where strength to face the challenge is gained, when medical personnel say something is going to work and it actually does.

As we waited for the results the rest of the lab results came in first. The white blood cell count was over four hundred thousand. The one done the day before was one hundred and ninety three thousand. (Normal is less than twenty thousand.) His white cells (which is where the cancer was) were doubling daily.

The bone marrow results revealed that it was ALL again—acute lymphoblastic leukemia—the same kind of cancer Justin had battled before. This was strangely comforting news. It could have been a worse kind of leukemia or more than one kind. At least this was a familiar foe and one he had been victorious over before.

We thought we knew ALL, but this kind of aggression was new to us. Healthy blood cells were competing with immature, useless white cells for space within the walls of Justin's bones. Leukemia is a battle waged in the most concealed part of the body—the bone marrow—where all the elements of our blood originate. Red cells, white cells, plasma, everything that is essential to life comes from within our bones. The leukemia cells had to be stopped, or Justin would die in a matter of days.

He was sent to ICU in a wheelchair. Continued blood tests showed that his white cell count was increasing so quickly that by that afternoon it was already over half a million. As we settled into the ICU, the intencivist greeted us again, only this time he was more serious, almost apologetic. He knew we understood the seriousness of his presence, and he had been right. I didn't want to need him. Dr. Sato was there too. They needed to start getting some of those leukemic white cells out of Justin's bloodstream immediately, or his body would start having serious organ failures.

His blood was getting so thick with immature white cells that it was becoming sluggish, making his kidneys, liver, and heart work much too hard. A peripheral intravenous line was started in both of Justin's arms. Gel-padded leads were attached to his torso with thin, black wires connecting him to a heart monitor. A pulse oximeter was placed on his finger to measure oxygen saturation levels, indicating whether he was getting enough oxygen.

A leukapheresis machine was wheeled in. A giant, blue box on wheels, it would remove white blood cells directly from Justin's blood. When counts get high enough to cause hemostasis or "sludging" in the capillaries, this was the machine to fix it. In my years of working as a maternity nurse, I had never seen one of these. It looked a bit like a respirator, and it scared me. An empty IV bag was hanging above it. A technician came in and attached one of Justin's IV lines *to* the tubing leading into the machine and the other IV line leading *from* the machine. There was little discomfort. The three of us watched TV and adjusted to the new surroundings. Within the hour, the empty IV bag began to fill with white blood cells, peachy white in color, like chicken broth. Before long, it was full. The white cell counts began to drop within hours. The critically high counts were now under control. Justin started to feel noticeably better. The swelling in his jaw diminished. It was instant gratification at its best. I loved that big blue box.

I asked, "Can't we just keep doing that? Suck the leukemia cells out of him?"

"It only works temporarily. Not for the rest of his life," was the response.

Now that Justin was more stable, a central intravenous line needed to be placed as soon as possible again in order to infuse chemotherapies too toxic for smaller veins. Like when he was five, central line meant easy access for withdrawing and infusing blood again. There was urgency because of the aggressive nature of the leukemia. Everything was happening quickly. We watched as our boy, now on the brink of manhood, wearing a blue hair cap and a hospital gown, was placed on a gurney, no longer the little five-year-old who lay in that position nearly ten years before. He was wheeled past the double doors leading to the surgical suites, away from our reach. Seeing him carted away wasn't any easier than it was when he was little. In fact, it was tougher knowing that the brutal nature of the treatments he would wake up to; the intravenous catheter protruding from his chest, the nausea, swelling, weakness, body aches and eventual hair loss from chemo would be Justin's to bear without the naiveté of a child. This was his body and his mind and his spirit experiencing the full force of this combat; and this time he had to do so with the knowledge and perspective of a semi-adult. Dave and I held each other, our heads together, shoulders jerking up and down as we cried in disbelief.

Our family and friends came. They sat with us, walked the grounds with us, cried with us, prayed with us, and helped with the girls and baby Jacob, who was just four months old. I cried and cried at the sense of helplessness I felt. Dave and I coped best by sharing our misery with others. This time, we knew firsthand what the chemo would do. We knew about the changes in appearance, the mood swings, the depression, the isolation, and we knew it would be tougher on a teenager. Jessica was eleven years old. Joelle was six. They looked up to their big brother with such reverence that it made my stomach ache and my throat tighten to think of the pain they were in and of the neglect they would soon experience as their mother and father disappeared into the fog of a war being waged within their brother's bones.

Upon Justin's diagnosis, I was nursing a four-month-old baby. If I was away from Jacob for more than three hours, my breasts would swell like water balloons and start to leak. This was a nuisance at first, because breast-feeding in an ICU was not exactly conducive to mother-baby bonding. Whenever Jacob heard a beep or a new voice he would turn his head to take a look, leaving me exposed and sore. At the same time, nursing him calmed me in the way that a glass of wine or a purring kitten induces relaxation. The weight and warmth of his soft body against mine quelled my panic and took me to another maternal place all together.

Since Justin's last battle, we'd been given nine more years to know, absorb, and love him, and there was nothing I didn't like about him. I wanted a lifetime more. Sometimes I wondered if it would have been easier to deal with his suffering if he were a rotten kid.

Experiencing the relapse was kind of like finding out I was going to give birth again. The first time you go into labor, you are naïve. That innocence is a blessing. You shore up for the unknown pain ahead. You can't imagine how difficult it is going to be, so you prepare yourself mentally, physically, and spiritually as best you can. Through prayer and meditating on Scripture, I prepared myself for Justin's birth: baby number one, textbook; baby number two, stressed out but a quick delivery; baby number three, I told Dave, "I'll kill you if you ever do this to me again." Baby number four, an epidural. But there was no way to numb this pain.

With Justin's original diagnosis, I believed I'd been chosen, set apart for this kind of challenge, and I accepted it. I'd been a nurse long enough to know that bad things happen to good people, like the three-year-old boy I took care of in nursing school who had been disemboweled by his own father in a drug-induced rage. He lay there, asleep, eighteen puncture wounds marking his soft, smooth skin. What had this toddler done to deserve this kind of death? He was good people. I didn't ask, *Why me?* or *Why Justin?* Instead, I asked, *Why* not *me? Why* not *my Justin?* Were we so different from the rest of the human race that we should somehow not have painful experiences like this? I was spiritually sound, and that was good. In those early years, I felt confident that Justin would be healed. While it might have been naïve, that kind of thinking made it easier to live with. I had prayed for Justin to be healed, and for a long time, he was.

This time was different. His relapse meant we would likely be faced with a bone marrow transplant. I recalled visiting the transplant unit at CHLA when I was job hunting a year out of nursing school. Kids sat in beds alone while lab techs and loved ones reached through floor-to-ceiling-length clear plastic curtains with gloved hands, unable to touch skin to skin, the patient looking more like an unfinished porcelain doll than a person. Bone marrow transplant for ALL patients is reserved for non-responders, those whose leukemia does not die with chemo. If Justin's did not succumb to chemo like it did the first time around, then transplant would be the last resort and the chances of him surviving were slim.

I knew I would have to leave my job as a mother/baby nurse at the local hospital and take care of Justin as I had done before. His central intravenous line, a Hickman catheter, was a bifurcated tube about eighteen inches long. Six inches lay under his skin, and the rest dangled from Justin's chest. About a quarter of an inch thick, the white tube had two lumens with caps, which had to be changed weekly using sterile technique. The Hickman had to stay dry at first, and only showers were allowed later, which meant, as before, Justin could not go swimming or take a bath. It was important to maintain the IV site properly, as it could be a source of infection. Dressing changes involved exposing the site every couple of days. Administering IVs, keeping track of oral medications, lab results, appointments, home schooling, and managing side effects like nausea, vomiting, hair loss, muscle soreness, weakness, and depression were all part of it. At this age, Justin would be more in tune with his body. This time he would also know everything he would be missing. His spiritual needs were his own. He would have to face God in his own way.

As Justin's chemotherapy began, there was concern about tumor lysis syndrome, which occurs when too many white blood cells (WBC's) are destroyed very quickly. The levels of byproducts like phosphorus, potassium, and uric acid become so high that they cause kidney failure. These changes could also cause a drop in calcium, which could lead to heart arrhythmias and seizures. With leukemia, the blood itself *is* the tumor. Most people think of a tumor as something solid, something that can be cut away. Leukemia patients don't have that luxury. It cannot be sliced out, sewn up, and tossed in a biohazard bucket. This was a tedious, delicate operation, one that would take time and a close and watchful eye.

The day we arrived at City of Hope, arrangements were made for us to use one of the apartments across the parking lot. They were for patients or families who lived too far away to commute. I could stay close to Justin with the baby and have a place to sleep while Dave stayed the night with Justin. Jess and Jo could visit and stay the night too.

The day after our arrival, the girls came to see their brothers. Jessica sat on the bed with Justin. Joelle and I went for a walk in the rose garden. I detested being separated from them and had to use this visit to prepare the girls for what was ahead. The roses had been freshly pruned back to their stumps and looked more like skeletons than bushes. Joelle noticed that each of the bushes had metal nameplates poked into the soil with names like Dolly Parton and Red Devil.

She said, "Mommy, are dead people buried here?"

I laughed and held her unusually strong little hand. "No. Those are just the names of the rose bushes. And in a few months, they will be full of blooms. There are no dead people here."

"Is JD going to die?" she asked.

"I don't know," I said, swallowing hard.

"If he does, I'm glad the Red Devil isn't buried here."

I agreed and gave her hand a squeeze.

She walked a little farther and found some dandelions. She picked one and blew the white fluff away.

She said, "I'll bet you know what I wished for."

I squatted down, facing her, my hands on her hips. "For JD?" I asked.

"Yep. I'm wishing for JD to get all better."

"Jojo"—I looked at her petite, pretty face—"that was a very good thing to wish for." Hugging her, I said, "I'm so glad I have you."

Standing, taking her by the hand, we started walking back to the hospital, passing massive oak trees and metal sculptures across the expanse of lawn to the fountain and the wheelchairs I'd seen with Justin the day before. We made our way back to the entryway. Stepping inside, I looked toward my Jojo and wished I could take all of this away, but deep down I knew that when it came to defeating Justin's cancer, it would take a lot more than a mother's desire and a little sister's dandelion wish.

On Golf and Mystery

Three days after the relapse, I found myself lying on twin beds pushed together in the family apartment at City of Hope, forty-five miles from home. Baby Jacob, warm and soft, lay next to me, nursing. I never imagined myself having another baby at the age of thirty-nine. Jacob's birth had been unplanned; and as I gazed at the bleak backdrop of the dull linoleum floor below, I wondered why he had been given to me against the odds of birth control. I hated having to be there—Jessica and Joelle with Nana and Grandpa, Justin across the hospital parking lot with Dave. Like a mother cat, I wanted to pick each one up and carry them back to the safety of my nest, but I couldn't.

Mornings are harsh when cancer has your child by the throat. I felt tired. I was anxious and lonely, and I could feel the muscles around my throat tensing within minutes of wakefulness. I had to do something to slow my thoughts. Prayer was my Xanax. I repeated the one scripture still within reach of my memory: "For God has not given us a spirit of fear, but of love, and of power and of a sound mind" (2 Timothy 1:7 NKJV). *Not a spirit of fear, not a spirit of fear, not a spirit of fear, a sound mind, a sound mind*—my mantra. I held onto those words tight, reminding myself that I, indeed, was not timid, had authority, and a sensible mind. This I needed to repeat often as I struggled with believing it.

I looked around the stark apartment and felt a bit better seeing the things my sister Lori brought the day before: a floral quilt, soft towels, pillows, and snacks. It did my heart good to have a few comforts from home, knowing that there were women around me who would be there every day from here on out as my life became centered on keeping Justin alive. Any thoughts of him going to school, graduating from junior high, attending family parties, taking vacations would wait again; and I ached at the thought of it.

Justin had just been released to an oncology bed, making this his first morning out of ICU in three days. I picked up the phone and called his room.

"Did you get a little more sleep this morning? Is your IV a little less sore? Are you feeling better?"

"Yeah."

His voice cracked one-word answers. In typical adolescent form, it fluctuated between uncontrollable high and low tones.

"Does Papa like it better there?"

I couldn't tell whether he was smiling on the other end of the phone; so I asked Justin to hand the phone to Dave, who still loved being called by the name Justin gave him as a toddler, the more endearing name for father: Papa.

"They just finished moving him, and he is already enjoying his new room. It has a nicer TV, and there aren't so many monitors alarming all the time. When is Lori coming? I need clean underwear."

Dave sounded upbeat.

Before I left the house, I'd grabbed enough diapers and onesies for Jacob but had not packed enough clothes for myself. Now that Justin was stable, my mind began to engage in practical thinking, which, prompted by my noticeably embarrassing stench, meant I needed a shower. I didn't want to take Baby Jacob over to the hospital, so Lori agreed to come and sit with him.

Relieved to have been able to nurse him through the night and still be close to Justin, I was thankful for the proximity of the housing and my sister. I'd spilled tomato soup from Justin's dinner tray the first night here on the only pants I'd packed; and since I also forgot to pack pajamas, I had to sleep in soupy sweat pants and a breast milk-stained T-shirt. I felt more than ready for a shower by the time she arrived with my fresh clothes, but I just had to see Justin and Dave first. I handed Jacob to Lori, splashed water on my face, and ran across the parking lot to the main hospital.

When I got to Justin's new room on the oncology wing, he was sitting up, smiling, finishing breakfast. It was a private room—a luxury in most hospitals. Its plain, outdated white walls, linoleum flooring, and faux wood bedside table were of little importance. A large window covered by gray, stained vertical blinds made for a bleak backdrop except for the sunlight that leaked in between the cracks. As prison-like as it appeared, the independence from the cramped quarters and multiple monitors in the ICU was liberating for Justin. He was down to one IV line in his left hand and looked less puppetlike.

When I entered the room, Dave told me that a social worker had just come by to ask Justin if he wanted to meet Kathy Ireland. Justin had no idea who she was, but Dave, remembering Sports Illustrated swimsuit editions past, lit at the offer. She was visiting City of Hope and wanted to spend time with some of the pediatric patients.

"I told the social worker we would be there," Dave said with a grin.

"I'll go take my shower and be right back," I said.

"No. We have to go right now," Dave responded. "They want him in the teen room right away."

"Justin, are you up for this?" I asked.

"Yeah. Going for a walk sounds good."

Always agreeable; that was Justin.

I didn't want to miss out on any of Justin's experiences; so I sighed and popped a piece of gum in my mouth, the polite thing to do, considering that I hadn't even brushed my teeth. Oily hair, sticky hospital skin, unshowered, in my tomato soup pants and a milky shirt, I surrendered my pride and agreed to meet an infamous icon of feminine beauty.

We walked from the inpatient hospital to the outpatient tower next door. The corridor to the teen room was also the corridor to the outpatient clinic. It seemed like a lifetime had passed since we'd entered those wooden doors three days prior. Justin pushed the IV pole and walked slowly but steadily. Dave, his arm around Justin's shoulder like a blanket, walked next to him. My heart ripped open at the sight of them. They were so comfortable with each other, so at ease. Justin liked everything that his Papa liked. There was never a struggle between them. A few steps behind, tears welling at the sight of the father-and-son blend I loved so much, scratching at the stain on my pants, I followed them into the teen room.

Several other kids were already sitting in the cushioned chairs. A little girl maybe five years of age, thin and pale, wearing a floral scarf over her bald head, giggled and told knock-knock jokes. Sitting next to her were what seemed to be her parents. Another teenage boy sat slumped and did not smile. His baseball cap was worn low on his brow, and it left the back of his hairless head exposed. Justin pushed his IV pole next to a soft recliner and sat down. It is odd being in one room with so many sick kids, strangers caught like ill-fated fish in an unyielding net.

The sun peaked through the vertical blinds and warmed the chilled room. In a short time, Kathy entered as an entourage of people in suits and ties crowded the doorway. Regal and tall, her highlighted brown hair fell in stylish ringlets around her flawless face. Her perfectly pressed, gray slacks; crisp, white blouse; and high-heeled, black boots were the perfect ensemble. A cameraman followed her as she went around the room and greeted each of the kids with a warm, gentle hug. A large, padded microphone hovered over her every word.

When Kathy greeted Justin, he stood up like a wobbly colt and smiled his bright, toothy grin.

"Wow. What a great smile," Kathy said as she shook Justin's hand. "How are you doing, Justin?"

"Good," Justin said as he always did.

His one-word answers made me tense. I wanted to tell them how sick he had been just three days ago, how close to death he had come, how hard his life would be now; but this was not my time to be heard. It was his.

"Do you like to play sports?"

Shuffling his feet and looking away, he gave a timid, "Yes."

And then there was a lag. I wanted to say, "Yes, he likes sports. In fact, he loves sports; he played flag football at last year's Turkey Bowl. And don't forget basketball. He could dribble when he was barely two years old. Mountain biking, hiking, and rock climbing. He loves it all." I didn't know how many times Kathy had done this, walked into a room full of kids liable to die before their next birthday. I admired her willingness to do so but at the same time wondered about her motives.

In the midst of the hiatus, a deep, rumbling voice from the back of the room surfaced.

"Hey, Justin. What's your *favorite* sport?"

It came from a man who towered over the group and was the tallest, leanest man I'd ever seen in a suit, tie, and dress shoes.

Justin paused for a moment and shrugged his shoulders. I thought for sure he would say, "Running," since he had been a cross-country runner with a local youth team most of his life—that and Dave being the high school track and cross-country coach, it seemed the natural response; but he didn't.

He perked up and said, "Golf! I like golf."

"You'll have to come to the tournament," Jim said.

And then Kathy asked, "Justin, do you know why we're here?"

"No," he replied.

"We are hosting a golf tournament."

"How'd you like to play with the pros?"

Justin's eyes opened wide as his smile grew.

He responded without hesitation, "Sure!"

I couldn't believe it. Was this for real? From ICU to a golf tournament in thirty minutes or less? Was this a recipe for disaster or the sweetest deal Justin might ever receive?

As the group mingled, we found out that the Kathy Ireland, Greens.com Classic, an LPGA tournament fundraiser for City of Hope, was to be held in South Carolina that May.

I walked over to Kathy and introduced myself. When we shook hands, I felt like Pigpen meeting Lady Diana; but her kind smile put me at ease.

"Thank you for helping the kids," I said, crossing my arms over my milk-stained T-shirt.

"It is the least I can do," she said. "Justin is so handsome. His smile is amazing."

I liked her but still felt a sense of curiosity about what motivated her to be there. Where did her strength come from? Did she know someone who'd had cancer? Why do strangers like her work so hard to help children? It seemed strange to me that Justin was surrounded by so many enthusiastic people who were willing to step into his life in a positive way so immediately. On this disordered morning, I was guarded as we mingled in the teen room. But seeing the smile on Justin's face alleviated some of my anxiety. I watched as the people from Kathy's team mingled with Jim's and excited conversations over Justin's enthusiasm for golf ensued. I was still stunned that he said *golf* without having any idea why all of these people were here. I knew that something bigger than all of us was at work, and I began to care less about the stains on my clothes and more about the mysterious nature of the day's events.

The tall man approached us and began writing down our contact information so that arrangements could be made for Justin to play in the tournament. Jim Etzel was the Executive Vice President of Business Development at Greens.com and the owner and founder of SportsOne Inc.—a sports and entertainment development company. His deep voice and casual demeanor were not what I'd expected from a businessman—no stuffy, white-shirt-and-tie standoffishness or cool, calculated conversation. This guy was for real. He put his arm around Justin's shoulders, which met Jim at hip level.

Looking up, Justin asked, "How tall *are* you?"

"Six eight. And don't worry, Justin. I get asked that a lot."

Sometimes people say things to sick kids and then walk away, never to fulfill what they have implied. Not Jim. The company he represented would handle our travel arrangements and everything else we would need in order to participate. He was one of those people who you feel you've known your whole life even though you've just met. He made direct eye contact, nodded and listened when we spoke. He made us feel like the most important people in the room even though we were complete strangers.

In the middle of questions about how many airline tickets we would need, the IV monitor alarmed its annoying *Bling-bling! Bling-bling!* Lost in thoughts of golf games and travel, the shrill sound slapped me back to our reality. The tournament was three months away. Justin had just gotten out of ICU. Even if he could play in a few months, the flight to South Carolina could be impossible for a kid on chemo; or would life itself pose the greater impossibility?

It was decided to begin the same treatment plan that Justin endured when he was five. Because he had been in remission for so long, that this relapse could be treated like it was an initial diagnosis. The déjà-vu of beginning the same exact treatment regimen seemed cruel. Lab results revealed that the leukemia was responding well to the initial treatments. Remission was obtained, and two weeks later Justin was discharged with the understanding that his treatments would continue at City of Hope, just as they had at CHLA, on an outpatient basis. Coming home was like landing on an island after being adrift for weeks. Thanks to my family and friends, the carpets had been sterilized, the linens washed, and the hand sanitizer placed by the front door with a box of surgical facemasks. Someone even wrote a note asking visitors not to come in if they had cold symptoms. They had been through this with us before, and their expertise showed.

Having to do this again—the chemo, the blood transfusions, the platelets, the long drives for treatment, the isolation from friends—I hated all of it, even the hand gel. The spontaneous lifestyle we enjoyed for almost ten years was gone. The uncertainty of surviving was insufferable. I loathed having to battle this beast again but tried to hide any negative thinking from my family and myself.

Upon returning home, concerned friends and family began calling as news of Justin's sudden relapse and then new remission circulated. Explaining to friends and family the details of treatment and what remission meant was exhausting.

"Why did it come back? What happened?"

I didn't know why. No one did.

"He's in remission again. That's good right?'

I explained over and over again that so much time had passed between original diagnosis and relapse that Justin's medical team had decided to treat him as though he had never had leukemia at the age of five, which meant he could receive the most potent regimen. That remission while on chemo was a good thing, but now we had to wait and see if he was able to maintain remission while on treatment. People like solid answers when they are afraid. They wanted to hear me say that everything would be okay, that Justin would be fine, like he was before; but there was no certainty in what I had to say and repeating it so much felt like I was a cheerleader for an underdog team, and I didn't have much time or energy for that.

So I began screening phone calls. Time management is a vital skill when you have a sick child. I needed people who offered help with the day-to-day chores and who were good listeners. Very few people want to hear how bad treatments are. I know too many families who have been abandoned by their closest friends and family members because they get worn out.

Dave and I took turns driving to the outpatient clinic at City of Hope. Like most parents of kids with cancer, whether medically trained or not, you become your child's nurse, advocate, and spokesperson. For important appointments, we went together—the ones where treatment plans were discussed. Dave was better at remembering the details, like percentages and numbers. I was better at understanding the physiology and concepts. We were a team, but being the nurse always meant I would be in charge of Justin's hands-on care. I tried to keep a positive front. I had to, but I was scared. Watching Justin wince when I had to peel off the tape from his hairless chest; swab his IV site with dark, orange-tinged Betadine; and then replace the dressing over his tenderized skin, I didn't want to be his nurse. I just wanted to be his mother.

As a family, we were still adjusting to having a new baby in our midst. Years ago, I'd scoffed silently when I had patients who were having babies in their late thirties and early forties. I never wanted to be having a baby and be that *old*. Dave and I had picked the name *Jacob* when I was pregnant with Joelle, if she had been a boy. As we were faced with the possibility of losing the big brother, the first-born, the one who anchored us, I found it mysterious that the name we chose for our youngest meant *supplanter*.

We began taking the daily trips for treatment. We had Jacob's blood drawn to see if his bone marrow was a match for Justin, just in case. Within a month, Justin's hair started falling out. When he was five and this happened, it all came out at once in the bathtub.

This time, he fingered it while watching TV or talking on the phone and sort of played with it by pulling off dry clumps. It was like a dog shedding. Hair appeared on his pillow, the couch, the headrest in the car. Eventually, he shaved off the stragglers. Dave shaved his head too. My dad, my brothers, and all of my uncles were naturally bald, so Justin became the youngest skinhead in the family. His face and belly swelled from the steroids, and his arms and legs atrophied to skin and bones. The teenage muscles he had just developed disappeared. He looked toad like yet handsome. His smile remained.

The side effects from chemo were much worse than when Justin was originally diagnosed at five. At one point, he developed pleurisy, which caused severe pain in his chest when he breathed. His cousin, Lauren, six days younger than him, rushed with us to City of Hope, holding his hand and trying not to make him laugh—impossible when they were together, which made for an interesting hour-long drive.

"Lulu, stop it," he cried with a bent smile.

Another time, he was sitting in the big, green chaise in our front room, watching me paint the living room wall. Painting seemed frivolous, but home projects were my therapy.

He said, "Mom, my heart is beating really fast, and all I'm doing is sitting here."

Justin rarely complained. I put down the paintbrush and took his pulse. His resting heart rate was 130 beats per minute. Dave was at work. The girls were at school. I grabbed Justin by the arm, put Jacob in his car seat, and sped off to City of Hope. There were emergency rooms closer to home, but I'd learned that when you have a kid with cancer, you go where people know you and you know them. It's safer that way. City of Hope's urgent care would be open. Chemo kills good cells as well as bad ones, so walking into a public emergency room would have been like letting Justin swim in contaminated waters.

When we got to City of Hope, it was determined that too many healthy red blood cells had died. He needed to be transfused. He received two units of blood that day.

The fear of losing Justin was chronic. Prayer was constant and global; and like a salve, it helped. For almost ten years, I was the parent who would walk in the oncology waiting room, look around, see all the bald kids, and think to myself, *I am one of the lucky ones. My kid beat it!* Not anymore.

Sitting in the infusion room day after day, I wanted to know if the child in the next seat, with IV tubes coming from underneath his shirt too, had what my child had. If so, was it their first time? If not, how many times had they relapsed? If it was their first time, I knew they certainly didn't want to talk to us.

"What are you in for?" one parent would say to another; they were like cellmates.

Sometimes I wanted to tell people around me that it was back; but other times, I just wanted to isolate myself. And so I'd read, watch a movie, or play cards, all the while wondering how we got into this reformatory in the first place.

One day, Dave, Jacob, and I sat with Justin in the IV room. Dave offered to get us some lunch. When he returned, his forehead was furled.

"I met this woman in the elevator. It was strange." Then he pulled me aside and said, "She asked me if the boy with the big smile was my son. I told her he was. I asked her if she had a child there on treatment, and she said she'd had a son around Justin's age but that he had died."

"Did he have leukemia?" I asked.

"No, but she said that she also lost a daughter several years prior. She was there visiting the nurses. She said those were her only children. She wished me well, said she would pray for Justin, and stepped off the elevator."

I was accustomed to the fear of losing Justin, but the thought of losing another child had never occurred to me. It seemed too unfair, too cruel. Why would this woman come back to City of Hope if she didn't have to? How could she find enough faith to pray for a stranger when she carried such immense pain in her own life? I looked at Jacob napping in the stroller, next to Justin's chair, his soft, brown hair stuck to his sweaty forehead, his chest rising and falling, and his thick toes motionless. Dave and I looked at each other, knowing what the other was thinking: *Could this happen to Jacob?* But there was no room for that kind of thinking. Not now. We still didn't know if Jacob was a bone-marrow match.

As the date of the golf tournament approached, Justin was in the second phase of therapy, which meant he had to be monitored closely. He was back in remission for now, but it was important to keep up certain levels of chemo to keep the leukemia cells from returning. It was a balancing act between keeping just enough good cells to sustain life and wipe out as many bad cells as possible without killing him. Justin clung to the hope of playing in the tournament as the cancer treatment continued.

It seemed so backward to try to save Justin's life by killing him one cell at a time again. The tug of war playing in my heart was more intense this time around. I resented the treatments more for making him visibly suffer. I began researching alternatives. It made me angry that ten years had passed since his original diagnosis and the exact same chemotherapies were being used. Little had changed. The only difference was that cranial radiation, which he had endured at age five, had been eradicated from the arsenal. It had eventually been proven not to improve outcome.

As if having leukemia twice wasn't bad enough, Justin had also contracted hepatitis C through a blood transfusion when he was five years old, the days before it had a name, when it was called non-A or non-B. We received a letter in the mail three years after the transfusion. It had remained dormant all these years, but it meant that his liver functions had to remain within tolerable limits or treatment would have to be altered. Every time he had a blood transfusion, all I could think was, W*hat about new unforeseen blood-borne diseases? Would he contract something else that might kill him, something nameless hiding beneath the surface?* He was receiving blood transfusions every week. Family and friends donated blood, but there were no guarantees that the faces we knew and loved had spotless blood to match. Blood does not lie.

Blood Brothers

When it is your kid who has someone else's life essence swimming through his veins, it is like you're in a boat, watching your child swim in the ocean. All you can do is pray that nothing surfaces to swallow him.

The time had come. It was Thursday, and we still didn't know if Justin would be able to go to the tournament. We were supposed to leave on the following Monday. Jim was waiting for us to confirm. There was nothing Justin wanted to do more. Dr. Sato was pensive. It all depended on the latest blood draw. His blood counts had to be just right in order for Justin to be able to travel and to allow a one-week pause in chemotherapy.

Even though I'd hoped that Justin would be able to make it to South Carolina, I tried not to build up the idea of playing in the tournament. At that time, he couldn't even eat a fresh strawberry for fear of infection; but he was supposed to be able to get on an airplane, fly across the country, play in an eighteen-hole golf tournament, mingle with the pros, and then fly all the way back to California without getting sick—all the while protected by an immune system that functioned about as well as life raft full of holes.

He has not given me a spirit of fear. He has not given me a spirit of fear. I had to hear myself say these words over and over again in order to believe them.

On good days throughout treatment, when Justin had the strength, he'd play golf with Dave. It was one of the only sports he could still participate in while on therapy. It was an outdoor sport, so it did not increase his risk of exposure to infection. It was non-contact, and it was not overly strenuous. He could play even if his blood counts were somewhat low. He loved golfing with his Papa. It kept his spirits up and made up for the fact that he couldn't run anymore.

Considering Justin had only experienced a couple of group lessons in his lifetime, he was a natural. He was very patient and had a knack for the ball. His stroke was smooth and purposeful. He was small in stature, so what he lacked in power he made up for in finesse. The tranquility of the sport matched Justin's personality. After being invited to the tournament, he was determined to play as often as he could. Sometimes he was so weak when he was playing that when he squatted down to pick up his ball, he'd have to use his club like a cane and push himself up. Chemotherapy destroyed his muscles, but the game lifted him up and out of the dark underworld of cancer therapy and onto the open greens.

The lab results were in. His red blood cell counts were borderline low, which meant he couldn't receive more chemo for at least a week even if we stayed home; but miraculously, his cell counts were high enough to be stable enough to fly. Dr. Sato gave Justin the thumbs-up along with a blood transfusion, and we were on our way.

The girls were thrilled to be on an adventure with their big brother. Sometimes siblings are so damaged by the time their brother or sister with cancer recovers or dies that a family suffers loss on many levels. To be included in this trip made them a part of the adventure. The flight was uneventful. Justin grumbled a bit when I made him wear a portable air purifier around his neck.

"Just pretend it is a necklace," I said.

"Mom, it does not look like a necklace. Do I have to wear the mask too?"

He didn't like wearing either of them, but in classic Justin style, he did what he had to do, put a smile on his face, and focused on the prize: the tournament.

We arrived in South Carolina at around 9:00 p.m., picked up the rental car Jim had arranged for us, and drove the long, dark highway to Myrtle Beach and then to a beautiful plantation-like complex at the Wachesaw East Country Club and golf course. Our townhouse overlooked the fairway, complete with an expansive front porch; locally crafted, high-back rocking chairs; and two screened porches. The kids ran through the house and up the stairs, choosing which bed they would sleep in: the twin beds with matching quilts for the girls; and for Justin, the cozy bed on the screened-in porch closest to Dave and me. It was dark when we arrived. In the morning, it seemed that green was everywhere. The lush forest surrounding the property was fairy tale-like. Red cardinals fluttered about like common sparrows.

Traveling posed more activity than Justin had seen in weeks. Dave and I were tired, but the kids tickled each other and laughed. I called home to see how Lori was doing with Baby Jacob. I didn't like leaving him for so long at this age. He was only seven months old. I had started weaning him before we left but still had the occasional let down of breast milk whenever I heard a baby cry or thought about how much I missed him.

I consoled myself knowing that at least Jacob would be too young to remember my absence. Besides, being able to spend much-needed time with the girls and attend the tournament without Jacob crying in the middle of a tee off was well worth the sacrifice of leaving him behind.

The morning after our arrival, Dave and Justin were up at six o'clock. I thought for sure Justin would wake up with a fever or a weird rash or some terrible pain in his chest. To my pleasant surprise, my son with leukemia was up and ready. I flushed his Hickman IV catheter, put on a fresh gauze dressing, and wished him luck. He donned his new tan golf shirt and white golf shoes—a gift from Greens.com and Kathy Ireland Worldwide. He covered his bald head with his favorite Titleist cap and slipped a bright, white golf glove in his pocket as though he'd been playing in pro tournaments all his life. Father and son could not have been happier.

Thanks to Jim, the girls and I had our own golf cart. We were allowed to be on the course, but I knew nothing about golf etiquette and would have been mortified if I screwed up a player's game because I drove up to the green at the wrong time.

"We have to be very quiet when we get there," I instructed the girls, who giggled and strapped themselves onto the rear of the cart and pretended they were golf bags.

"Come on up here, you two."

"Ah, Mom, can't we ride back here?" they asked.

"No. But if you come sit next to me, you can take turns driving until we get to the course."

We met up with Justin on the seventh hole. He and Dave were paired with Jim and professional golfer Nancy Scranton. Justin had his own golf cart too. Even though it was not allowed in tournament play, Jim had made arrangements for a local pro shop owner to drive the cart for him in case he became too tired to walk. He walked the entire course just like everyone else. Cancer was not the victor today.

Justin inexplicably was making every putt. Nancy hit the long shots; and since they were playing best ball, it became apparent that Justin should hit most of the short shots. He was making one birdie putt after another. He appeared poised and confident, his swing smooth and easy. Nancy was genuine in her enjoyment of him. Not everybody has the ability to step into the life of a sick child. Nancy did it with grace, as did Jim and Kathy, strangers unaware that the gift Justin was opening that day would provide an unforgettable experience not only for him but for those of us who experienced it as well. Justin never stopped smiling.

Some people have the incredible ability to know what you need before *you* do. That was Jim. "Want a drink?" he'd ask at one stop and then, "Are you hungry? Lunch is in the clubhouse. Let me take you there." His hardy laugh, long stride, and lanky swing made him endearing. No wonder Justin bonded with him so closely that day. I don't know why I expected Jim to be distant and aloof. I suppose it was because he was a white-collar man, and I mostly knew blue-collar people. I could not have been more wrong. At one point he picked up Jess and placed her on his shoulders for the highest piggyback ride she'd ever had, and she fell in love.

There were about fifty spectators lingering as we reached the ninth hole. Nancy once again teed off and placed the ball on the green. The heat and humidity were getting to the girls, who threw themselves onto the grass and gasped liked fish out of water on several occasions. Justin seemed unaffected by it.

Nancy started asking Justin for advice.

"Hey, Justin, can you give me a few pointers on how to putt like that?"

She had played in hundreds of Pro-Ams and had never seen anyone putt as well as he did that day. Confident, he stepped up and made a beautiful thirty-footer on a double-tiered green right into the hole. Cheering erupted. Justin glowed.

On our way to the tenth hole, we were told that Kathy wanted to see us. We hopped in our carts and were escorted into the hospitality tent. She looked sporty and cool, untouched by the South Carolina heat, her pale blue, plaid shorts and white-collared shirt perfectly pressed. Her thick ponytail hung from the back of her crisp, white golf cap.

"Hi, Justin. I hear you're really ripping it up out there."

She was holding her two-year-old daughter, Lilly, on her hip as she reached to each one of us and greeted us with hugs. Cool drinks and warm company made us feel welcome.

Kathy and I talked for a moment.

"I met someone who knows you," she said.

I was stunned and asked, "Who?"

Since Kathy lived in Santa Barbara and I lived eighty miles away, in Santa Clarita, not to mention that she was the CEO of her own multi-million-dollar company and had friends in higher places than I could dream of, I couldn't imagine knowing anyone within her social circle.

"I went to my Tuesday morning Bible study," she said.

Bible study? I thought.

"A friend of mine asked for prayer for a boy named Justin at City of Hope." Kathy continued. "I told her that I'd met Justin at City of Hope a few months ago." Shifting her daughter to her other hip, she said, "Her name is Debbie, and she told me that she met Dave in the elevator there on one of her visits to see the nurses."

Kathy's friend Debbie was the woman in the elevator, the one who had lived through the loss of her only son and only daughter. What were the odds of a world-renowned beauty, a grieving mother of two, and me—a mom/nurse fighting for my son's life—converging under such dire circumstances?

Again the idea that something mysterious and powerful was at work here entered my mind, and I took notice.

As Kathy and I talked, I was surprised by her casual, unpretentious manner. I know this sounds prejudiced, but I was most astounded that she attended Bible study. I'd imagined that someone, with the life experience of a swimsuit model, and as accomplished as her would have little time for anything to do with Christianity. I had known so many struggling followers of Christ that it was a fairly new phenomenon to see someone so successful professing her faith.

Getting to know Kathy was like hanging out with an old friend. We quickly found out that her father and mine had attended Cathedral High School in Los Angeles. Her mother was a nurse and so was I. She was the middle daughter of three girls, as was I. What touched my heart most was that Kathy remembered my Justin in prayer. I felt a kinship with her as my preconceived notions disappeared.

As we returned to the green, I pondered the revelation that two women I'd never met who lived miles away from me in a community I knew little about, two women who met my boy briefly at City of Hope on separate occasions a hundred and fifty miles away from their homes, two women who showed up to a Bible study on the same day, chose to pray for my son. It seemed their lives were worlds away from mine. The reality that perfect strangers are brought together in ways unknown even to them astounds me.

I couldn't help but wonder why this was happening. Why was I supposed to know about Debbie? Would she help me if Justin died? Once again, I had to file that thought away. There was no room for it in the midst of the magic.

"Good luck out there, Justin. Keep up the good work." Kathy hugged Justin again.

Justin smiled, shy and gracious. "Thank you. Thank you for everything." He turned and headed back to the course.

I'd read in the paper the next morning that Kathy's involvement in the tournament had come with conflict. The confederate flag still flew over the South Carolina State Capital building. Lending her name to a tournament held there put her in the center of a struggle between the NAACP and South Carolina. The NAACP wanted her to back out of the tournament or she would be considered insensitive to the civil rights issues there. I wouldn't find out until months later that she personally called the head of the NAACP and told him that if she pulled out, the one most hurt by it would be a boy named Justin, who was fighting for his life. The response from the NAACP leader was one of kindness. Kathy's courage to speak up on behalf of my son made way for Justin to live out one of his dreams. It was as though the day's events had been written specifically for him.

Nancy continued to lead the game in best strokes and offer Justin drinks. At last we approached the eighteenth hole. Nancy landed the ball about twenty feet off the green, fifty feet from the cup. Dave took a try at getting the ball to the hole and missed.

Jim said, "Go for it, Justin."

The green grass glistened in the hot, moist air, spectators hushed; and Justin stepped up to the ball. As the crowd watched, he prepared his shot. He steadied his feet, covered in white leather and tassels; pressed the spiked soles of his shoes into the grass; and took a couple of practice swings with his child's set seven iron, his favorite club.

A shot like this with a kid's seven iron is impossible. Justin hit the ball, making a clean, solid *crack*; and a hush came over us all. The ball hopped onto the green and then rolled, curved right, continued to roll another fifteen feet, broke left, crept closer and closer to the pin; and finally, with a thump, landed in the cup.

Justin shouted, "Yes!"

Jim pumped his arm in victory.

Dave ran over to Justin, wrapped his arms around him, picked him up, and jumped up and down, laughing. "Way to go, big guy!"

Nancy shouted, looked skyward, threw her arms straight in the air, and let out a victorious, "Oh my god!"

Jessica, Joey, and I did a little happy dance on the edge of the green.

Justin's face lit up as he celebrated. As the foursome exited the green, he seemed to float to where children greeted him, eager to meet the kid who'd garnered so much attention on the course.

"Will you sign my ball? Can I have your autograph?" they asked, and Justin held a black Sharpie and signed one ball after another.

I had never seen him happier.

The word had gotten around about the boy with cancer who out birdied everyone at the Pro-Am. Wherever we went, people wanted to know if he was the one. The professional golfers greeted him with a handshake and asked for his autograph. ESPN wanted some footage and asked Justin to show off at the driving range for them, which he did gladly and thus fulfilled another aspect of his dream.

That evening, at the awards ceremony, under the cool, lit night and the clanking of wine glasses and silverware, Jim stood and quieted the crowd.

"Justin, would you please come up here?"

Their foursome had taken third place in the Pro-Am. Justin, wearing his mask, air purifier, and hat, walked toward Jim, who placed his long, slim arm around Justin's slight shoulders.

In his deep, calm voice, Jim began, "Justin is why we're here today."

Justin beamed.

"This young man has had to endure more challenges than any of us in this room," Jim continued. "Today, he showed what he is made of and hit more birdie putts than any other player, including the pros! He never tired and hit an incredible shot on the eighteenth hole. What I witnessed here today was nothing short of a miracle."

The crowd applauded.

"We can all learn from his courage. Justin, you are my hero." He paused and handed Justin the clear, crystal, etched trophy. Justin held it close with his bony fingers. His smile was brighter than I had ever seen.

The crowd stood up and gave a standing ovation.

As I stood among the crowd, the feeling of awe over the inexplicable way Justin played was overwhelming. The thought occurred to me that he had done more living that week than most people do in a lifetime.

The local pro shop owner who had driven the golf cart for him and seen his juvenile clubs firsthand brought him a top-of-the-line putter from his shop the next day, cut to size and customized with a new grip. He couldn't believe this boy had accomplished so much with so little.

"My life will never be the same," he said to Justin. "You made me a believer, man."

Every day in America, someone somewhere is working hard to grant a wish for a terminally ill child; and no doubt had Justin made his wish to play in a professional golf tournament known, it probably would have been arranged for him. But no one did know, and no one could have made that ball do what it did.

Buried deep in the rough of Justin's life, a silly game of hit and miss lessened the pain. In the thick of it all, witnessing such triumph gave me the feeling that everything was as it should be. Seeing Justin in that light gave me a sense of peace that rose to the surface of my heart, spilled into my mind, and lifted my soul. I wondered if this was what the psalmist meant when he wrote, "My cup overflows."

Lisa Solis DeLong

Nothing Sacred

If arriving in South Carolina was the beginning of Justin's dream come true, then leaving was the beginning of his own personal nightmare. We'd had such a great time in Myrtle Beach that we didn't want to come home. It had been a retreat from the reality of cancer clinics and sickness. I wanted to continue seeing Justin off of chemo, embraced by Southern hospitality, playing the game he loved, but no one wanted to let the South Carolina dream continue more than Justin.

When it was time to pack our bags and head for the airport, I went upstairs to get Justin's Hickman care done and wake him up, but he was already awake. He was lying on his back, his arm folded over his face, weeping harder than I'd ever seen him.

"I don't want to leave. I don't want this to end."

I put my hand on his shoulder. "I'm so sorry, Justin." My vision was blurred by tears, and my throat tightened. All I could do was lower my head to meet his and agree. "I don't want it to end either."

Going home meant we would fly five hours to Los Angeles International Airport and then drive another hour straight to COH (City of Hope).

Our plane came in late, so we missed our connecting flight. We were going to be stuck in Dallas for a long layover. Justin looked weary, and I worried about what his immune system was being exposed to by hanging out in a bustling airport. I begged the girl at the counter and explained our situation. I played the leukemia card, and she managed to book us on another airline. We were on another plane in an hour. Arriving in Los Angeles later than originally anticipated, our luggage was delayed by several hours. We filled out the necessary paperwork and went home weary. The only plus: it was too late to go to City of Hope.

The return to clinic trips and chemo and labs and the long waiting periods began again. The miracle we had experienced in South Carolina seemed to carry us through the next month. It helped to ease the disappointment when we received the news that Jacob was not a bone-marrow match for Justin. I already knew that the girls were not, and I felt cheated because I knew of families who only had two children and they matched. Here, I had four, and none of them could help keep Justin alive. This realization reignited my quest for alternatives. I had Justin's medical records sent to the Immune Institute of Orange County for a phone consultation I had scheduled with a physician there. I prayed for guidance when she advised me to bring Justin to see her.

She said, "I believe we can help Justin."

I asked how many pediatric leukemia patients they had treated before, and she recited a case of a little girl who lived out of the country who had been cured. I asked if I could speak to her parents.

She said, "We used to be able to put people in contact with them, but they requested not to be bothered anymore."

Was this a scam, or was it the answer? I prayed for discernment and wisdom and scheduled an appointment.

July third, Justin's fifteenth birthday, was fast approaching. His life had changed so drastically since his fourteenth birthday that I didn't know whether to celebrate or mourn. He was feeling pretty good some of the time but had bouts of terrible headaches, nausea, and muscle weakness. He needed something to look forward to, but I didn't know what to do. Planning a party would mean knowing the future, believing there would be a day to celebrate—like buying a crib before a baby is born, but I couldn't make that commitment.

Every day was an uncertainty, but I wanted to do something to cheer him up.

One sunny afternoon on the way home from COH, I turned to Justin, who was sitting in the passenger seat, quiet, thoughtful, slumped low in his seat, looking out the window.

"Hey, Justin, you're only about a year away from driving. Are you looking forward to it?"

"Yeah," he said, looking at me, grinning. "Why?"

"Oh. I don't know. I was just wondering." I pulled off the freeway and into the large, mostly vacant LA Zoo parking lot.

"Mom, what are you doing?"

"You said you were looking forward to driving. Why wait? Here." I said, handing him the keys.

"Now?" He grinned.

"Yeah. Come on over here," I said, feeling like I did when he was five and I handed him a lollipop.

He hopped out of the car and came to the driver's side, sat down, and moved the seat back just an inch or two.

"Go ahead. Turn it on," I instructed as I buckled my seatbelt.

He smiled and started the engine. He placed his hands on the steering wheel, adjusted the mirrors, looked over one shoulder, then the other, and looked straight ahead. It did my heart good to see him like this—so alive. He accelerated with cautious spurts and then made a turn.

"Don't forget to look over your shoulder," I said, looking over mine. I looked around for any police cars and imagined getting pulled over. Perhaps I would need to play the leukemia card again, but I didn't care. He was too young to have a driver's permit but not too young to die. This was one moment I didn't want to miss.

We practiced parking and backing up. He started getting cocky and we headed toward a turn. Instead of slowing down, he sped up.

"Take it easy there, Mario," I screamed and held onto the door grip.

He punched it and spun the car into a whipping turn as though he had been driving for years. I screamed, and he laughed. This spontaneous, age-significant moment put a smile on his face I will never forget. It was as if cancer held the hourglass while grains of sand slipped through the opening and for a moment it lost its grip. In that space between what was and what will be, that minute sector of time known as *now*, my son was both transitory and interminable.

As July approached, we still had no plans. Until Jim Etzel called. He remembered that Justin's birthday was coming up. "I'd love to come see you all again."

Jim flew in on Friday. Seeing him again meant that everything we had experienced in Myrtle Beach was real. He had experienced the miraculous nature of the event too and was there to bear witness. I was in awe of his continued kindness toward our family. Dave, Justin, and Jim played golf all the next day. Jessica decided Justin should have a party for his birthday. I was too frazzled to even think about it anymore.

She called Justin's friend, Leanne, "Can you call Josh and Jesse and some more of Justin's friends to come over for a surprise party? My dad took him golfing, and they will be out all day." Within thirty minutes, Leanne had ten people coming over. Jessica and I baked a cake. When they returned home, there was a house full of friends; and they all enjoyed meeting Jim, hearing his stories about how amazing Justin's putts were, and gawking at his height. Thanks to Jessica, it was a great day.

Jim had an early flight out on Monday morning, July third, Justin's birthday. Dave and Justin were going to COH that day even though it was designated as a holiday for the Fourth of July, the clinic was open. I opted to stay home with the kids and clean up after all the festivities.

Dave and Justin dropped Jim at the Burbank airport and continued on their way to the clinic. I enjoyed being at home with my girls and little Jakie. My heart was lighter than it had been in weeks, still lifted by the fact that Justin had such a celebratory weekend. I was thinking about making him Grandma's casserole, one of his favorite dishes, for dinner.

At around two o'clock the phone rang. It was Dave. I expected him to say the usual: Justin's counts were good, he needed blood, they want to see him again Wednesday; but his voice was different, flat, dead.

He said, "Something is wrong. They want us to see the on call doctor about Justin's lab results. I'm afraid they found leukemia cells again."

Oh no, I thought. I had no words. I listened and wished I had gone with them.

After we hung up, I waited by the phone on my knees, rocking back and forth. As soon as I heard Dave's voice again, I knew.

"They found leukemia cells."

Justin had relapsed. Was this some kind of a cruel joke? Was this level of injustice allowed simply to add drama? Justin had been feeling so good and so happy. Today was his birthday, for crying out loud. Was nothing sacred? I prayed and begged for it not to be so. But pleading got me nowhere. His cancer was back on his fifteenth birthday. I felt a kind of helplessness like I'd never felt before. I wanted to be there where I could read Justin's face and ask his doctors questions.

Justin was admitted to the hospital again. That night, the nurses felt so sorry for him that they went out and bought him his favorite meal, In-N-Out Burger. They got him a cake and sang him "Happy Birthday."

"We will come home in the morning," Dave said.

We both knew everything had changed. Now that the chemo wasn't working, it was time to try what the Immune Institute had to offer; but I knew this would not go over well with Justin's oncology team. I was afraid of the confrontation we needed to have. I loved Dr. Sato and the skilled, kindhearted staff at COH; but when chemo stops working, you look outward. If we waited much longer and pounded his body with more chemo, we would hit a point where anything else we tried wouldn't have a fighting chance. His body would be too depleted. Even if the outside therapies were effective, they would work best if he was stronger physically.

Justin was released for the Fourth-of-July festivities. We met with my sisters' families and watched the fireworks being launched into the dark sky from the Valencia Town Center parking lot. The firecrackers burst into spectacular displays of red, white, and blue overhead. I stared at Justin's face as it lit up and then, disappeared in the darkness between blasts. Justin tried hard to make the best of the moment; but there was a look in his eyes, a knowing, a lack of twinkle. His smile was less vivid. He did a better job of disguising his fear than I. All I could think about was the next Fourth of July; would there be one, or would this be our last one together?

Justin and Dave went back to the hospital that night. We met with Dr. Sato and a doctor from the bone marrow transplant team the next day. These are when the big guns come out—the experts. They explained that a transplant would be Justin's best option. It meant that he would be given two rounds of very heavy chemo that would basically wipe out his entire bone marrow. He would then be placed in the transplant unit and given bone marrow from a donor. As we faced the reality of searching the National Marrow Registry in order to keep Justin alive, I felt robbed.

Preliminary screenings done through the bone marrow registry revealed that there were seven potential matches in the world for Justin. Two were in Europe. The transplant team likes to start out with at least ten. I called the doctor at the Immune Institute and told her our predicament. I had not been able to keep any of the appointments I made there because something always happened so that I had to take Justin to City of Hope instead. Either his counts were too low and he needed a transfusion or his appointment took longer than usual; something always stopped us.

Now, sitting with these doctors, hearing them describe how risky the transplant was and what Justin would have to endure—mouth sores, vomiting, complete separation for at least a month, and threats to every organ in his already strained body—I just hated the thought of it. I never looked at transplantation as the answer. It seemed barbaric. To completely annihilate your own natural defenses; possibly destroy vital organs like the kidneys, liver, or heart along the way; and then introduce somebody else's essence, did not sit right with me. I knew that transplants could cause terrible rejection syndromes, extended suffering, and ultimately lead to death. I knew kids who had experienced just that, so this imagery was not fictitious. Again, the reality that treatments might kill Justin was beyond my ability to embrace. I just couldn't accept that it was the best way to go.

While bone marrow transplants have been glorified in the media, I knew in my heart of hearts that if Justin went for transplant, he would die. I told Dr. Sato that I did not like the idea of transplanting and that I wanted to try the Immune Institute first.

"Would that be a viable alternative at this time?" I asked.

"Waiting to begin transplant puts Justin at greater risk of transplant failure."

"What would happen if Justin died from the leukemia itself instead of the therapies?"

"He would bleed out," she said.

At this juncture our options included: potential death by high fevers, sores on all mucous membranes and intense pain, or death by blood loss as it oozed from every orifice of Justin's body, giving new meaning to the saying "pick your poison."

She looked me in the eye and answered each of my questions factually and compassionately. This is what I liked about her. There was no second-guessing. She knew her stuff. I had to trust her.

"It would be best to prepare Justin for transplant by starting the harder sequence of chemo while the transplant team looks for donors. This way if they get him back in remission and find a donor, he will be able to have the transplant. If his body does not respond to the stronger therapies and does not go into remission again, then I will agree to try other options."

Dave and I succumbed; we would follow what Dr. Sato recommended, but I had to ask Justin what he wanted to do. He was the one who was face-to-face with his maker on this. He was not a little boy anymore.

I asked, "Justin, what do you want to do?"

He said, "I want to go to the Immune Institute. I like the idea of trying to build up my body for the fight and not hurting it."

He understood himself. I explained what Dr. Sato had said and that we would try it if this next round of chemo didn't work; but in my heart, I felt like I had betrayed him. It was my idea to try alternative therapies. I'd made them sound grand; but the simple act of taking him there now, his platelets low from chemo, the leukemia cells on the rise, would put him at risk of bleeding out or infection on a daily basis.

I could not stand the thought of losing him without ever knowing what he thought about his life, not being one to say much, always covering his feelings with a smile. I needed to have an intimate conversation about death with my son even though I knew it would be difficult. I couldn't stand the sound of video games and movies anymore. I decided to talk to Justin about dying. I might never get this chance again. If he survived, I reasoned, we could look back and laugh at how his mother dragged his emotions through the gutter at his lowest point.

I sat next to him in the bed, put my arms around him, and said, "Justin, can we talk?"

"Sure," he said, clicking off the TV.

"Why do you think all of this is happening to you—the golf tournament, meeting such wonderful people, and now relapsing again?"

He lowered his head and then lifted his eyes to meet mine. "I don't know. I'm confused by it."

I waited, silent, determined to hear him; and then he said, "I feel like I'm running a race, the hardest race I've ever been in. And as I get closer to the finish line and I think all this pain and hard work are almost over, someone moves the finish line."

My throat tightened, but I did not cry. I did not want to make his pain worse. The last thing sick kids want is to make their parents cry, and I didn't want him to stop talking to me.

"Do you feel like you are being punished?"

"No. Not really. I mean, why would God let me have so much fun at the tournament if he was just being mean? I know he is there, but I just can't figure out why it had to come back. That is what I'm confused about, doing this over and over again."

"Do you ever feel afraid of dying?"

"Nah, not really, I don't think about dying that much."

"If you do, I want you to talk to me. I don't want you to be afraid. Justin, you know we are all going to die someday. You know that, right? I'm going to die, Papa is going to die, Nana and Grandpa are going to die, Jessica and Jojo are going to die, even Baby Jacob is going to die someday."

He lowered his head again.

"No one knows the time or the place, and people don't like talking about it. But you can talk about it with me."

He looked at me and then down at his hands. He fidgeted with the blanket and listened.

"Justin, you're fighting cancer, and it's hard not to think about death. But the truth is, one of your friends could step off the curb and get hit by a car tomorrow and you could live another sixty years. We just don't know what's ahead. I don't want you to think about all this stuff alone. You can talk to me about anything. Right now, we know that miracles happen. Look at what we experienced in South Carolina. Hold onto that."

"Yeah. I know, Mom. I'm not confused about that," he replied with a little grin. "Maybe I'll end up being a pro golfer."

"Maybe you will. Wouldn't that be something? Promise me you'll talk to me if you have questions."

"I will. I promise. I'm really not afraid, Mom."

This is how most kids with cancer get through the day to day. They often have a quiet acceptance. Justin focused on his video golf game and phone calls to friends, while Dave and I fretted over the impossible task of granting his request to try alternative treatment while staying within the confines of a working relationship with the medical professionals we had trusted for so long.

If we stopped all chemo now and went to the Immune Institute, we would be going against medical advice. This meant that if Justin needed to return for a blood transfusion or any emergency services, there would be no guarantee that our insurance would cover it. It would also put strains on our relationship with everyone caring for Justin and make their treatment regimen more difficult to manage. If this aggressive cancer started running rampant again and we showed up at their doorstep, they would have to start all over again. He would be in a much worse state, and I would be responsible. I even had concerns about the legality of taking a minor away from approved medical treatments to unapproved. When a parent goes against medical advice they can lose the legal right to parent anymore. I made an appointment with the Immune Institute and explained to Justin that all we could do today was follow Dr. Sato's advice for now.

Justin was to have a ten-day course of hard chemo, have a break for about five days, and then return to the hospital for another round. During this time, he and I and Dave were able to spend a lot of time with each other. Once again, family and friends stepped up and relieved us of many of our duties at home. It was summertime, so the girls had more freedom in their schedules; and Jacob was almost nine months old and becoming less of an infant and more of a toddler.

I loved hanging out with Justin. Holding his hand, lying in bed, he was affectionate, patting the space on the bed sheet next to him, whether at the hospital or at home, indicating that he wanted me to be near him. He made me feel welcome, wanted, and well received even in his most difficult moments, never pushing me away. When he was awake, I enjoyed playing a Nintendo golf game with him. He was really good at it, and I stunk. I know this because he told me so in his croaky voice.

"Mom, you're not very good at this, but don't worry. I'll help you."

He explained all the little tricks that made the ball go farther, and acquire more loft; then, he reached over, jiggled the joystick, and guided my hand to land the ball just where I needed it. Eventually, out of frustration, he took the controller out of my hands and moved the joy stick with much more finesse than I ever could have. He quickly pushed the buttons while chewing on his tongue the way he did when he was young, all the while laughing at my ineptness. I thought he was just schooling me in a childish game to kill time between treatments. What I didn't recognize was that, in truth, he was teaching me about having the time of my life.

Lisa Solis DeLong

Let Him Go

Just one blossom of the blue hydrangea was big enough to be a bouquet. I admired them at City of Hope, where they grew along the wall next to the apartment parking lot. I originally noticed them back in February when Justin relapsed the first time. Hydrangeas don't grow well where I live in Santa Clarita. They don't like the hot, dry summers or the frigid winters; and when they do survive, they usually resemble deflated purple balloons. At COH their periwinkle blue puffs were the size of basketballs. I thought they were spectacular. Whenever I needed a break from the bleak hospital walls, I'd walk up to them, cup my hands around their soft, blue petals, and study how each stem was really a masterfully crafted cluster of hundreds of dime sized flowers. Individually they would have gone unnoticed; but put together, they offered me rich inspiration.

Many times I drove up to the apartment, saw them and thought about picking some, drying them upside down, and taking them home. *A memento of our stay,* I would think. I imagined myself in the future, looking back at Justin's time battling cancer, at how difficult it had been; and in my mind's voyage, he would be sitting next to me as a man. The dried hydrangeas, discolored and fragile, would sit inside a vase on a corner table, a distant reminder of how tragic the outcome might have been.

Justin was asleep in the apartment, and I'd rather have cut off my right arm than disturb him in the midst of his much-needed sleep. I took a blanket to a field of freshly mowed grass under a giant oak tree outside of the apartment. The sky was clear and seemed bluer than usual. Maybe because I had not sat beneath it for a while. Maybe because after two weeks of the hardest rounds of chemo Justin had ever received, he got a break. Hospitals don't have sunroofs. I soaked up nature's beauty, all the while trying to make sense of the repulsive nature of the disease we were dealing with. I read my Bible, and prayed silently. When besieged by medical crises, there are few things more comforting than the hush beneath the arms of an aged, great oak. I wondered how many other people this tree has seen, praying silent prayers of hope and desperation.

I prayed that I would know what to do, that I would be given wisdom as promised in the psalms and proverbs I'd read over and over again.

Sitting there, I remembered that I had a pair of pruning scissors in my car. I snuck over to the hydrangea bushes, afraid that the gardeners would be displeased if I snipped a few. I picked five. Their thick stems cut easily, and I bunched them up in my hands and walked back to the blanket hoping that my daydream would come true.

In the aftermath of receiving chemo with names that sounded more like agents used in chemical warfare than healing—Vincristine, Ara C, and Cytoxan—it felt good to get away. For two weeks, these treatments had been brought in by nurses wearing industrial strength masks and gowns, and hazmat gloves up to their elbows to protect them against the carcinogenic side effects of the neon orange liquid they came to infuse directly into Justin's veins. I hated chemo. It saved Justin's life and gave us ten precious years, but that was over now. I hated that it made Justin so sick and fragile. He wasn't quite like walking death yet, but he was on his way. His mouth drooped to one side. I noticed that his smile was lopsided a few days prior; "A palsy of some kind," they'd said.

We opted to stay on the City of Hope campus with Justin after his heaviest rounds of chemo were finished and we were discharged. The list of potentially lethal side effects was long and subject to change. One list read:

> The following symptoms require medical attention but are not emergency situations. Contact your medical provider within twenty-four hours of experiencing any of the following:
>
> - Unusual bruising or bleeding
> - Black or tarry stools
> - Constipation
> - Diarrhea (4–6 episodes in a 24-hour period)
> - Nausea
> - Vomiting (more than 4–5 times in a 24-hour period)
> - Severe abdominal pain
> - Lip or mouth sores
> - Painful urination
> - Bone pain

Staying close made sense. We could get help in a moment's notice if need be, unless he needed help after hours. In that case, we had to call an ambulance to take him to a nearby hospital with an emergency room. COH was a wonderful place during the day; but late at night, you were on your own in the apartments. I had heard the sirens and seen the flashing red lights and a patient being carted away on a gurney more than once.

Experience taught me that new chemotherapies and higher doses meant the possibility of more severe side effects with little or no obvious symptoms and the need for quick intervention. Justin had not slept through the night in two weeks, as the chemotherapy he had been receiving during that time required twenty-four-hour intravenous infusions, which meant twenty-four hours of him having to urinate; that and the nursing assessments, lab draws, food services, and social workers offering everything from books to crafts. The interruptions never ended. He battled nausea during this time as well as fatigue. His nutritional intake was nil. No one seemed overtly concerned about either of these added stresses. We continued to offer Justin foods that he once liked, but now the thought of typical teenage favorites like pizza or burgers made him wretch. He took sips of soups and juice. In that two-week timeframe, we calculated that he had probably eaten less than a few hundred calories: two dinner rolls and some sips of juice and broth. His body was starving, and it started to show.

I was told that Justin had to be much more depleted in order to receive intravenous nutrition, known as TPN, because it too could have serious side effects; but I hated the helplessness I felt watching my son become so sleep and nutrient deprived, and said so. The nurses placed a note on his door. "Do Not Disturb," it reads. They tried.

By the time we got to the apartment, free from IV's and monitors, the first thing I did was unplug the phone and make Justin some chicken noodle soup. He ate more than he had in weeks: a half a bowl of soup and a few crackers. Exhausted from the wheelchair trip across the parking lot, happy to be out of the hospital, he took a long, much-needed nap. Dave ran errands, and I sat outside on the blanket.

I prayed for clarity about going to the Immune Institute the next day. I owned a cell phone by this time. Its ring startled me. It was Anush, a woman I'd met at a lecture by a doctor from the Immune Institute. Anush had fully recovered from liver cancer after following his recommendations, and she encouraged me to get Justin to the Institute. I told her we had an appointment at the Institute the next day; and to my surprise, she said, "I have an appointment there tomorrow too." When we hung up, I thought her call was my moment of clarity, my open door to taking Justin to the clinic the next day. It was the confirmation I needed, and a new hope welled up in me. I would be able to take Justin where he wanted to receive treatment and hopefully begin the process of offering him something restorative rather than destructive. I laid back; placed my hands under my head; and took a long, deep breath as tears ran down the sides of my face. The oak branches crisscrossed the open sky above me like great fingers entwined to lift me up; and for the first time in months, I was buoyed by hope.

That night, Dave and I pushed the twin beds together and sandwiched Justin between us. He was unfettered by IVs for the first time in what seemed like forever. We wrapped our arms around him and enjoyed the bliss of holding our teenager, the warmth of his skin, his feet bigger than mine; a remnant of evidence that his once muscular body was at the cusp of being more man than boy. We fell asleep easily like this, no alarms, no voices, no checking of vital signs.

But the sweet taste of sleep soured around 1:00 a.m., when Justin sat up suddenly and, in an urgent, cracking voice, said, "I have to go to the bathroom. I think I have diarrhea."

He crawled out of bed and didn't make it to the bathroom in time. This cycle continued every half hour or so until around three in the morning, when I called the doctor on call. Justin had received IV fluids before being discharged from the hospital, so I believed he was well hydrated and everything we'd read about chemo said that diarrhea and vomiting were common side effects; but I was concerned that the severity of Justin's symptoms were more than routine.

The on-call doctor said to give him another Zofran for his nausea and, "Keep an eye on him," whatever that meant. My eyes couldn't see his blood pressure; and without a stethoscope and cuff, I couldn't take it.

"If he develops a fever, bring him in right away."

No fever ever occurred, so I tried to let Justin and Dave sleep as much as possible between a couple more bouts of diarrhea. His pulse was a little fast, but it usually was these days. I considered calling an ambulance, but Justin drank some water and fell asleep for two more hours, so I didn't. I decided to shower and get dressed, still thinking that this would be the day that we would make it to the Immune Institute. The phone call from Anush had confirmed it in my mind. I believed that even though Justin had diarrhea, we would go to the Hem/Onc Clinic as usual, they would give him IV fluids, and we would still be able to drive to the Immune Institute in Orange County. I put on a fresh, white T-shirt; my favorite khaki jumper; and sandals. I was blow drying my hair when Dave got up. I put on a little makeup and watched Justin sleep, a peaceful, uninterrupted sleep. Dave felt his forehead as he had throughout the night.

"No fever."

Justin woke up and sat on the edge of the bed. He leaned over to put on his jean shorts and tried to walk but sat back down.

"I feel really lightheaded," he said; so we called for a shuttle to pick us up.

The golf-cart-style shuttle arrived, and he sat quietly between Dave and me. We helped Justin out of the shuttle at the entrance of the main hospital the way we always did when we were going up to outpatient Hem/Onc. They were expecting him. Dave grabbed a wheelchair, and Justin sat down.

In the Hem/Onc waiting room, Justin said, "Mom, I feel like I'm going to pass out."

I ran for help, and Dave wheeled him into the day hospital area, where one of the physician's assistants took one look at him in the wheelchair—he was leaning forward, holding his head in his hands—she called the medical team to help.

"He has that look," she said.

What look? I thought.

Just like when he was five and I couldn't see how sick he was, I couldn't see it until now. This is how it is in the mind of a parent when their child has cancer. There is a nucleus of fear in us so blinding that we cannot see what someone else who does not love them can identify in an instant. When I saw the symptoms and took immediate action, I felt like a hero; miss it and you feel like the world's biggest loser, totally undeserving of ever been allowed to have this precious child in the first place.

Justin's blood pressure was so low that they immediately began pumping fluids—blood, plasma, Ringer's lactate to restore hydration, bring up his blood pressure—and then they added piggybacks of smaller bags containing antibiotics, antifungals, and everything they could to fight infection. An hour later, a tired but smiling Justin rested quietly as a weary medical team wiped their brows. As hydration was restored, a fever erupted.

"Sometimes in the presence of severe neutropenia (an abnormally low number of white cells), a patient can have an infection without having a fever."

Dr. Sato told me this, but how was I to know this ahead of time? Without infection-fighting cells, Justin was at risk of a life-threatening condition called neutropenic sepsis. Without a fever, there was no fire alarm.

If I had known this in advance, I would not have waited until morning to bring Justin in for help. If I had known that a fever was not always apparent when a neutropenic kid was fighting infection, I would have called an ambulance at 3:00 a.m.; neither the doctor on call, my mothering experience, nor my nursing experience had prepared me for how quickly dehydration can occur in a well-hydrated teen or that the absence of fever did not guarantee that serious infection wasn't present.

Going through cancer treatment with a child is like walking in the dark holding hands with a stranger, one hand gripping your child and the other holding tightly to the firm palm of this person;

the person you have to trust, though they are blindfolded too, they seem to know the way better than you do, even to the cliff's edge as you're falling off of it.

Ridiculous as it was, it wasn't until Justin was admitted to ICU that it became apparent to me that we most definitely were not going to the Immune Institute that day. The khaki green jumper I'd put on that morning in the hope of being with Justin outside of the hospital, in the summer sun, heading away from City of Hope, seemed absurd then. My freshly groomed hair, the rosy cheeks—all of it was ridiculous. I felt like a fool and once again asked myself, *How could you not know how sick Justin was? How could you not see that he was ready to pass out? How could you?* I could practically hear the piercing, curt words from Dr. V ten years prior when he was originally diagnosed, "You nurses, you know how to take care of everyone else but your own kids."

I vowed never to wear that jumper again.

The ICU was as pale as its inhabitants. People in faded lab coats and multihued scrubs busied themselves at milky laminate desks. Phones rang and monitors buzzed as Justin was transported by gurney to the last room at the end of a row of about ten rooms. The reality of being there, in the same ICU where he had been diagnosed five months prior, was sickening. As we walked the length of the ICU, it became apparent once again that this unit served mostly adults. It didn't seem so bad that a gray-haired man with wrinkled elbows was lying in one of these beds or a woman whose age spotted hand revealed the excess of years she had already known the luxury of living. What ever happened to, "No kids allowed!?" Two rooms were reserved for pediatric patients in the ICU. One was empty, and the other was my son's.

Justin rested calmly, weak but appearing to improve. His color pinked up, and his vital signs stabilized. Dr. Arcenue, came by to check on him and to counsel us about what to expect with this episode. He wanted Justin in the ICU to monitor him closely since the newly developed fever might indicate infection. He used the word *sepsis* again. The chemotherapy, had wiped out everything his body needed to fend off invading cells. There were indications that this was what might have caused the severe diarrhea and the now-rampant fever.

Jessica and Jojo had gone to Tehachapi to stay with my mom and dad. It had become apparent that Justin would not be coming home for a while. Jacob was with, Lori. Dave and I sat by Justin's bedside, talking with him and holding his hand, helping him stand to pee into the awkward plastic urinal. He was weak and unable to stand on his own but didn't like lying in bed to relieve himself. Funny. It didn't seem all that long ago that he was a toddler, wetting his bed from time to time, attempting to potty train; and now, there he was, unable pee lying down.

The evening turned to night, and Dave took the first shift. We were a team playing tag, and he was it. I kissed Justin's forehead and took the long, lonesome walk across the dark parking lot to the apartment. Any other time, I would have felt uneasy walking alone in a parking lot late at night, but I didn't give it a thought. I entered the empty apartment where Justin had been with us, snuggled up together, the night before; and I felt a loneliness that was almost palpable, like a stranger in the corner of a dark room. I plugged in the phone, not wanting to miss Dave's call if he needed me. I crawled into bed. Exhausted but unable to sleep, I attempted to journal when the shrill ring of the phone broke the silence. It was my mom.

"I'm so sorry to be calling you this late, but Jessica is upset, and she wants to talk to you."

Jessica was crying when I heard her voice. "Mom?"

"What's the matter, Jess?" I took a deep breath and tried to suppress the lump in my throat. "Are you okay?"

"Mom," she sobbed, "I feel like JD is going to die."

She knew little about what had happened earlier that day. She knew we were going to have to stay at the hospital, but I'd told her that Justin was doing much better and that we hoped to be home in a couple of days.

"Oh, Jess," I said. "I'm so sorry, honey. You must be so afraid. Justin was very sick, but he is talking and smiling. I think he is getting better." I spoke with as much confidence as I could muster.

I could hear Jojo in the background, crying too. I tried my best to calm both girls as they took turns talking to me, but words came out in bits and pieces, and all we could do was cry. Still weeping, we said good night through little-girl whimpers and Nana's attempts to console.

Slumping into the bed, I hung up the phone, lowered my head, and sobbed, eventually praying myself to sleep only to be awoken a couple of hours later by another piercing phone call.

"Lees, you'd better come." It was Dave, speaking in the tone of voice I've come to know and dread: flat and serious. "He's having trouble breathing."

I threw on my sweats and ran across the even-more-desolate parking lot. Justin was wearing an oxygen mask now; speaking in muffled, weak tones; and his eyelids were heavy.

"I can't take ... a deep ... breath ... Mom," he said between gasps.

He was sitting up, obviously distressed. This I could see. His lungs were filling with fluid.

"Cough, Justin," I instructed as the nurse in me grasped for any productive action. "You have to get that fluid out and keep working your lungs. Cough, Justin. Cough."

"I can't," he said.

We sat him up even further and coaxed him to cough, then came clear, yellow fluid, the exact same color as the plasma that was flowing into his Hickman from the IV bag hanging on the pole next to him.

The nurse told us, "He is still receiving large amounts of IV fluids to fight the low blood pressure he is still battling. Dr. Arcenue is aware, and we are monitoring him closely."

This went on for about an hour; and then there was a settling, a calm as Justin began to breath more easily. It was my turn to be *it*, and Dave went to the apartment for some much-needed sleep. With no place to lie down, I leaned back in the plastic chair next to Justin's bed, put my feet up, crossed my arms, and closed my eyes. Justin's breaths came regularly, crackling through the port holes in the vinyl mask strapped to his face. Monitors hummed, pumps beeped, the room was a cacophony of strange and soothing sounds. I fell asleep.

They were resuscitating him in my dream, my handsome, fit, loving, and gentle fifteen-year-old son. I saw it all: the paddles, the intubation tube, the monitors screaming, the flat line. I heard the command to "give him epi." I saw Dave run to the entrance of the room, panicked at the sight. I held him back. The doorway was wide, trimmed in metal and glass from top to bottom.

"Let him go. Let him go. Let him go …" The words came out of my mouth with conviction, and then—

"Have a nice nap?" Justin's displaced voice met me as I awoke. He asked this question in his lighthearted manner, as if we were at home in our own beds and not in this jungle of tubes and towering IV poles.

Where am I? I thought for a moment, trying to focus.

"Yeah. A nice nap," I said, my mind reeling from the images I had just seen.

Searching for clarity, I focused on Justin's tired, deep, dark eyes I wondered what he was thinking while he laid there, pin-cushioned and taped, exhausted from weeks of torture, watching his mom in contorted sleep next to his bed. Could he see the terror in my eyes as the emotion from my dream lingered? He seemed peaceful, transcendent. The oxygen mask muffled his words but not his ever-present optimism. Oh how I miss his optimism.

The morning arose with little fanfare from those of us who had been up most of the night. It was a relief to see the sun in its consistent indifference to names or content of days. The clatter of charts and clipboards, quick-footed nurses, and lab-tech pokes brought in the dawn as Justin's blood pressure continued to falter and his lungs fought fluid for air. Dave returned after a few hours of sleep.

Dr. Arcenue pulled us aside, "His blood cultures have turned up negative so far," he said. "We might be dealing with something more serious."

More serious than sepsis?

"I'm concerned that Justin might be developing ARDS, adult respiratory distress syndrome."

I was familiar with the newborn version of this, which sometimes occured shortly after birth but was usually treatable. I was not familiar with the adult kind.

"I believe ARDS is what we are dealing with now. If fluid continues to fill Justin's lungs, we are going to have to intubate him in order to let his lungs rest."

We sat with this idea all morning, staring at monitors for signs of improvement. The phone rang in Justin's room.

"Is Justin there?"

It was Leanne Riggin, sounding like she did every day: bubbly, cheerful. She had an uncanny ability to reach Justin by phone there; and that day, she was a specialist.

Justin, barely able to speak, waved his arm, directing us to hand him the phone. Leanne talked, Justin smiled and mumbled beneath the oxygen mask. When he hung up, his arm fell in exhaustion.

His friend Josh Bush came to visit and, obviously frightened by the sight, still came in bravely and offered his hand to Justin, who held it with both of his. Josh left, and Dr. Arcenue returned.

"It's time," he said. "Justin is getting too weak. The respirator will do the work of breathing for him. He will be sedated so he won't fight the machine. We don't know how things are going to go from here. Some people with this syndrome survive, and some do not."

Dave and I held hands and stared at the doctor as though he wasn't there.

"You need to say whatever it is you want to say to Justin now. We don't know if he is going to come out of this. And once he is put on the respirator, he will not be able to talk."

These words, I tried to listen and take them in; but it was like someone had put cellophane over my ears, and I could only hear disjointed pieces of their meaning. This could not be happening, not to me, not to my boy. He was too good, too perfect, and too resilient. I couldn't believe this was real.

My brother, Ken, was there. His eyes were like giant blue-green reflecting pools. It hurt to look at him. When he was sad, they flowed with large, drowning drops. This was how he went in.

"I love you, big guy," he said. "You are my hero."

They shared loving and sweet words through giant uncle tears.

It was my turn, but I didn't want to go. Maybe if I waited a little longer, all of this would go away and Justin would get better; Justin would not have wanted me standing out there, shivering and afraid. Besides, he deserved better. I held Justin's hand, leaned close to his face, and kissed his cheek. He was getting weaker.

I whispered into his ear, "You're going to fall asleep now, my son. And when you wake up, you're going to feel so much better."

I started to cry, and I knew he was not going wake up there.

Dave's eyes reflected the fear and courage that only a father could know. He stepped close, leaned over, and hugged his boy. As I moved out of the way, he said, "I love you, big guy."

"I love you too, Papa," Justin whispered. "You're my best friend."

"You're my best friend too," Dave sobbed.

"It's not that bad, Papa," he said as we stepped away.

Making room for the intubation team as they enter his room, I felt a helplessness that was turning me inside out. I had to do something.

"We need to pray," I said to Dave and Ken, and we dragged ourselves into the vacant room next door.

As Dr. Arcenue sedated Justin and prepared to place an intubation tube into his trachea and the nurses followed his calm and skillful commands, I held hands with my brother and my husband and prayed the most earnest prayer of my life.

Lord, you know what is ahead for Justin. You know whether he will wake up from this only to endure more suffering, long suffering of more chemo, more nausea, more weakness, more loneliness, only much worse as he goes for a transplant. Father, you already know what is going to happen. If he is going to suffer through all of this, struggling to breathe, struggling to survive, only to suffer more and then die from this leukemia, please take him. Please spare him the suffering. Please don't let him suffer, Lord. Please don't let him suffer just to die anyway.

We finished praying together, the three of us. Dave exited the room and walked down the hall to the bathroom. Ken and I sat there, holding our heads in our hands as the hubbub of medical sounds coming from Justin's room intensified. And then it came.

"Code blue ICU! Code blue ICU! CODE blue ICU!" The operator's voice rang through the unit, practiced, clear, and cool.

"Oh shit!" I heard someone from the medical team yell as they ran toward Justin's room.

I looked up and saw Dave running past our door.

"Lees, what are they doing to my boy?" he screamed as he ran toward Justin's room, ready to pounce on everyone to defend his son from the pounding and pushing and physicality of their desperate attempt to bring him back. I lunged at him and held him.

And just as I had seen in my dream—the chest compressions, the doctor giving orders, the nurses filling syringes, and the cruel hum of the monitor—there it is was, the black screen of the cardiac monitor painting its telltale red line, flat and ugly.

I stood at the long, glass doorway, my hand on its cold, steel rim. I leaned forward and yelled, "Let him go! Let him go! Let him go!" three times.

Their heads turned.

Their hands stopped in midair.

They were in shock at my display.

But no one more so than me.

Wanting Him Back

When I was growing up, my family attended St. Finbar Catholic Church in Burbank. Going to Mass on Sundays, my two brothers, two sisters, Mom, Dad, and I would walk up the spacious, curved steps and open the heavy, wooden doors. Entering the foyer, we would line up to dip our fingertips in holy water, touch our foreheads, enter the sanctuary, and genuflect at the sight of Jesus on the cross. From there, we would file into a long, wooden pew with kneeling pads ready to turn down when needed. The high, open-beam ceilings and white, plaster walls made me feel small.

Often I would study the carved panels that depicted the Stations of the Cross and encircled the sanctuary: Christ carrying the cross, the crown of thorns, and women weeping while He died. The sight of Christ's plight held my interest more than the priest saying the mass in echoed words that I did not understand, partly because of the way the priest's voice bounced around in the church's poor acoustical interior but mostly because of his substantial Irish accent. I'd watch the white, flickering light of the prayer candles in their red, glass holders and wonder about Jesus being the true light.

My brothers, Rick and Ken, a few years apart in age, older than us girls, would pinch and poke each other until my dad would get mad and whisper, "God damn it, you two. Sit still."

Lori, Cathie, and I would giggle. Mom would lower her gaze at us, and we would try to regain composure. Being used to this routine, we'd watch as Dad pulled down the kneeling pads, brought his knees down, placed his elbows on the back of the pew in front of him, and leaned his forehead on his clasped, calloused hands. Watching and waiting until he fell asleep in that position, we girls would chuckle at our brothers as they began picking on each other again. Dad worked three jobs to keep us in our beautiful little Burbank home. It was no wonder he fell asleep.

From within the sanctuary, I could see the doors to the church confessionals that led to dark, closetlike booths, the sinner on one side of the inner wall, the priest on the other. A small window would slide open when the priest was ready, but he could not be seen through the one-way screen, where only his silhouette and his solemn voice were revealed. As a child, going to confession was scary. Once, after waiting in line to confess, when it was my turn to enter, the door opened and a little boy came out of the darkness, crying, his pants wet and a puddle on the floor. Not knowing what his sins had been and barely knowing mine, I still stepped in and took my turn, careful not to get my feet wet. As frightening as it was, my family was always waiting for me when I emerged, either kneeling or lighting a candle. I'd join them; and then, after I prayed my five Hail Marys and ten Our Fathers, as instructed by the priest, we'd compare our penance.

"How many did you get?" Ken would ask. He always had the most.

Church is what our family did together. I liked it. Some Sundays, if we behaved, we'd earn a stop at A&W Root Beer on Victory Boulevard. Nothing made me happier than being with my family and getting something sweet after being on my knees.

Years passed, and I left the Catholic Church when I was sixteen. Wanting a more personal relationship with Jesus and weary from the rituals of confession and Mass, through a Christian youth organization called Young Life, I learned how to commit my life to Christ. Becoming a born-again Christian meant not being Catholic anymore—at least that's what I was taught at the variety of new churches I attended. According to what I was taught by all my religious teachers past and present, a Catholic was not necessarily a Christian, and a Christian wasn't necessarily a Catholic.

Leaving the Catholic Church was not as bad for me as it had been for my oldest brother, Rick, who paved the way through our Grandma Solis's great disappointment. Even though all of us kids eventually left the Catholic Church, those roots are where I learned to honor the Father, Son, and Holy Ghost. From there came a longing to know more. I attended Bible studies for the first time where people did more than set their Bibles on coffee tables as focal points. They opened them up and read them, talked about the stories inside, and shared ideas about who Jesus was—the savior, yes, but also an ally. I soaked it up.

After Justin's passing, no amount of, "He's in a better place," or, "He's no longer in pain," eased my suffering.

Justin's death was too hard, and I wanted my boy back. The strength I found the day he died, when I prayed for God to end his suffering, was long gone.

A few weeks after the funeral, after picking the meat off of the bones of a whole turkey carcass and wishing those kind neighbors had sent Cornish game hens instead, after the nighttime bath for Baby Jacob and the tearful good night kisses from Jessica and Joelle, that night, when I finally laid my head on my pillow, next to Dave, the two of us in so much pain that we could feel it in each other's silence, I ached.

Our bed, once a sanctuary, was now a place of torture as sleep came only after replaying the whole ugly end over and over again until the Benadryl finally kicked in. The kids were upstairs—Jojo in the white, picket fence bunk bed I'd made her. Jacob lay in the oak crib which had first been Justin's. Jessica hid in her cluttered, preteen girl room—but Justin's room sat empty. I had nothing left inside to pick me up. No human being could comfort me. No book could explain what needed explaining.

I'd had enough time to let Justin's memorial sink in. We'd gathered on the track and field at Canyon High School, hundreds of friends and relatives walking the same chalk-lined, oval path Justin grew up on as Dave, his Papa, coached runners. We sat in the middle of the football field where Justin once played, eating fresh In-N-Out burgers. We lined up golf balls and hit in unison from the fifty-yard line. Food offerings were consumed, and so many mourners hugged me that my back ached and my mind reeled between joyous wonder at their turnout to excruciating pain for the reason. All the well-wishers went home, and after the casseroles and cold cut platters stopped arriving, when the flowers from standing arrangements started to dry up and the water in their vases began to stink and Justin's bed linens began to collect dust, that is when I knew death.

In the quiet of my bed, I wept, covering my face with a pillow to muffle the sobs. I heard myself muster up a silent prayer more from habit than faith. *Lord, please let me die in my sleep. Please end my suffering. I can't live with this much pain. I miss Justin so much. Please just take me in my sleep. I don't want to wake up to this reality again. Please, Lord. Please let me be with him.* I sobbed and sobbed and must have exhausted myself to sleep.

That night, I dreamed I was dying.

I could feel my breathing slow down, each breath a little shallower than the one before; and I was aware that my heart rate was slowing. I welcomed it. I was in a dark place, but I could see a circle of light, like the moon but closer. As I approached it, my breathing became ever slower, my heart rate an occasional faint thump, and then I saw him. Justin, as I knew him, was peaking over the edge of the circle of light as though he were looking down into a rabbit hole.

Blood Brothers

He said, "Mom, hurry! Come on! Hurry!" He gestured for me to come toward him like he had done when he was alive and wanted me to see a funny commercial or a new video game.

I came closer and closer to him, closer to the opening. My heart rate slowed and became ever fainter. I was so happy, joyful. I was going to see him, touch him, smell him. And then, nearly there, ready to go, Dave rolled over, snorted loudly, and woke me up.

I lay there staring at the ceiling, trying to decipher what had happened. Justin was so vivid. I thought about waking up Dave but felt too sorry for him. Falling asleep did not come easily in those days, and waking up was awful. But after a while, tossing and turning, I started to feel angry. It was like I'd hit the rewind button on the TV screen in my mind, and I couldn't turn it off, none of it—Justin's face, his voice, his death. I was mad at Dave for waking me up, and I would have smothered him with my pillow at that moment if it hadn't meant he'd get to see Justin before me. I wanted to see Justin even if it meant I really was dying. I tried to fall back to sleep, my only hope to tap back into whatever it was I had just experienced, tossing and turning, painfully alive. I never fell back asleep that night and never experienced that dream or that reality again. *Was it really Justin? Why did he want me to come to him? Did he need me? What did he want me to see?*

These kinds of dreams don't leave. They stick around, tapping on your shoulder from time to time.

A few months later, I began reading anything I could get my hands on about heaven. I read *Heaven: My Father's House* by Ann Graham Lotz and *Ninety Minutes in Heaven* by Don Piper as well as Randy Alcorn's *Heaven*. I began gleaning enough imagery to gain some strength back. I was slowly becoming more accustomed to Justin's absence but I needed to confront my grief more directly. I wanted to have conversations with people who were willing to talk about how bad loss felt. I decided to attend Compassionate Friends, a support group for grieving parents. My neighbor, Diane, was the chapter leader. She lived one house away from me in the home where she raised her two children. I hoped Diane could help me face my grief the way she had.

I remembered the day she found out her daughter, Michelle, died. I was standing in the front yard, gardening, as I often did back then, while the neighborhood kids ran up and down our cul-de-sac, chasing the ice cream man or shooting each other with squirt guns. A car pulled in front of Diane's house that day. She got out of the car, wailing, unable to walk on her own. A man held her by the elbow and gently walked with her across the manicured lawn to her front door.

"One of Diane's kids must have died," I said to Dave.

"How do you know?" he asked.

"No one cries like that unless their child has died," I replied.

How I knew this back then was only speculative. I wish it still was.

I believed sharing stories with Diane, whose daughter had died in a car accident, and others like her would help me manage the memories I had by getting them out. When I attended for the first time, it became apparent that I was right. Mothers and fathers of all ages shared horrific stories of their real life loss, which made me feel less isolated. Very few people have the capacity to hear the details surrounding the death of a child, but these folks did and their repeated gatherings helped me as I replayed mine.

When I was the one returning home after sitting with Justin's body in the ICU, and then after leaving the hospital, I sat on the lawn at City of Hope for I don't know how long. Not long enough, not wanting to leave, knowing it was over, hoping to fade into the grass and enter the soil beneath it. My sisters and friends gathered our belongings, including the blue hydrangeas, which I have to this day. As they emptied the borrowed apartment, Dave sat with me for a moment and then lifted me to my feet and led me to the car. When I got home, there was Diane. She hugged me and wouldn't let go.

At the meetings she led, I could talk about how I'd stroked Justin's hand, stared at it, waited for it to move, until his warmth disappeared. I didn't want to leave his body. I talked about how I'd held Jacob as he wiggled on my lap, trying to get out of my arms and onto the bed where Justin's body lay. How, after guiding Jessica and Joelle in to say good-bye—my two little, brown-haired girls, standing at the side of their brother's dead body, tears rolling down their smooth cheeks—I was numb. How awkward it was to be there for family and friends who came and went, solemn and tearful. How if someone hadn't eventually said it was time to go, I'd still be there.

Diane had been placed in my life to help me survive.

Often, when Jacob and I were home alone, my grief was most intense. One day, after Dave and the girls left for school, I sat on our wooden floor cross-legged, head sagging, staring at Justin's portrait. Jacob toddled around me. I thought about how I didn't want to love Jacob. I even vowed silently that I would take care of him but not love him. I never wanted to hurt that much again. I had no idea how much time passed as I sat there. I didn't care. As I sat numbly staring, Jacob crawled on to my lap, and I hardly noticed as my eyes remained fixed on Justin. Without warning, Jacob raised his right hand and slapped me across the face. "Ouch! What was that for?" I asked.

He giggled, grabbed my face with both hands, and blocked my view of Justin, as if to say, "You still have one son here, Mom. Pay attention to me." I hugged him, held him tight, and sobbed.

As the days lingered, I thought about Kathy Ireland's friend, Debbie, the woman in the elevator whom Dave had met at City of Hope. Kathy and Greg, her husband and an ER doctor, invited our family over so the kids could meet. I was in desperate need of family time, but our family did not feel the same without Justin. Everywhere we went, we ached through the motions of eating, sleeping, walking around. At Kathy's, we felt a twinge of light heartedness. Her family welcomed us with gifts for each of the kids. We brought a framed photo of Justin and Kathy that was taken at the golf tournament. It felt good to be somewhere new, where there were no memories of Justin and yet he was remembered. We reminisced about the golf tournament, ate sandwiches by the pool, and drank cool mango smoothies thanks to Greg. I needed to replay the end of Justin's life, and Kathy and Greg were open and willing to listen. Greg was the sounding board I needed, as his medical expertise helped me make sense of what happened in the final hours of Justin's life.

As the afternoon ended, I asked Kathy if she would contact Debbie for me. I knew I needed her now. I wanted to surround myself with other mothers who lived without a child; and Debbie had shown the strength to not only survive double losses, but she also exhibited an ability to thrive when she returned to City of Hope. The simple task of bringing cookies to the nurses there, speaking to Dave in the elevator, and sharing her story garnered my immense respect and curiosity as the pain I was experiencing was beyond what I could bear alone. This is what grieving people need: inspirational mentors, new memories, and good listeners.

Six months after Justin's death, Debbie came to my house with photos and an audio tape of her son Eric. We sat on the back patio and wept as we shared stories about our fifteen-year-old sons; about how smart, handsome, and good they were and how unjust it was that after surviving the extreme hardship of a bone marrow transplant after fully recovering Eric died months later as a result of pneumonia. But it was the sound of Eric's voice that touched me most as I realized it had been months since I'd heard Justin's. I considered the idea of watching our home videos, but the images and sounds of happy, healthy times were too much for me to bear. I could not gather the strength to look at them. It would be like taking a magnifying glass at high noon, opening my chest cavity, directing the intensified rays of light at my heart, and thus searing my raw flesh. I could not do that to myself; not then and not now. Debbie was so brave to come and visit me. Eric had been his little sister's bone marrow donor when she went through transplant years earlier, when he was still well and she was not. Debbie's willingness to share the pain of her losses, as well as the insights into her honest struggle with her faith, gave me hope that I could do the same. Her faith in Jesus was still alive. Holding onto her story is what got me out of bed on those mornings when I did not feel like I had the strength to do so.

Even so, at the end of the first year, I wanted to hold Justin in my arms more than ever.

In the midst of wanting him back and the reality that he was not coming back, no matter how many support groups I attended or how much crying I did, I formed a question. If he's not coming back, where is he really?

As a Christian, I believed in heaven; and I wasn't supposed to grieve as one who had no hope, but I felt hopeless. In another support group I began attending, hosted by the Michael Hoefflin Foundation for Children's Cancer (MHF), I met a woman who shared that six weeks after her eighteen-month-old daughter had died she was still getting up every morning, believing that her daughter's life would be given back. Not being able to touch, feel, smell, or hear your child is shocking. It can make you crazy. Like her, I needed tangible images of what heaven looked like, what it smelled like, what people did there. I needed to know if dogs and cats existed there, if flowers were present. I thought about Justin all the time: while driving the girls to school, while shopping for groceries. Once in a while, I'd see a young man with a flattop haircut and I'd forget for a moment and think it was him. I thought about Justin while paying the bills and cleaning the house, trying to fit him somewhere in my mind and not forget that he was real. I was living the adage: grief is love with no place to go.

One afternoon, a year and a half after Justin's passing, I received a phone call from Dave's nephew Randy Bittle.

"Hi, Auntie Lisa."

I was only six years his senior. At six feet tall, tattooed, pierced, and burley, his calling me "auntie" sounded funny. I giggled. He worked as a sound technician on the show *Beyond* with psychic James Van Praagh.

"Something happened at work today," he said. "I think Justin might have tried to come through during the show."

I had to lean against the kitchen counter. I immediately recalled what I had been taught by every teacher of Christianity I'd ever met or studied: *Stay away from psychics and mediums.*

Randy continued. "I was squatted down in the audience, holding the mic in the section James was focused on, when he said, 'Someone is coming through here, a young man. He's showing me his memorial, a memorial at a track and field stadium.'

"I wanted to raise my hand," Randy said, "but I couldn't because I was working the mic, but I think it was Justin."

I didn't know whether to laugh, cry, or hang up the phone.

"I know how you feel about psychics," Randy said, "but I just want you to know if you ever want James to come to your house and give you a reading, he said he would, and we could tape it and use it on his show."

Oh great, I thought. *I'll fall into sin and do it on national television!*

I thanked Randy, hung up the phone, and stood there in my kitchen a pile of dishes in the sink and a boatload of thoughts in my head.

I thought about Randy's offer for days and struggled with my theology. Of course I would love to meet someone who could reach Justin for me. What mother wouldn't? But relying on a spiritual medium, I imagined, would be like opening a portal where evil spirits could pour directly into me. Perhaps I had seen too many head-spinning, green-vomiting, spooky, male-voice-in-female-body movies as a teenager. Had I fallen so low that I needed *this* kind of help to make sense of things? What would it be like to have a reading?

When I was in my teens, my mom had thrown out our Ouija board after it had accurately instructed us where my brother's truck could be found days after it had been stolen.

"Ay no!" she exclaimed; mumbled something about, "*Diablo*," in Spanish; and tossed the board in the trash. A neighbor of mine mentioned once that she trusted psychics, but she'd left her husband for another woman and was later thrown in jail for being drunk and disorderly. I was not ready.

Time passed, and the need to make sense of the psychic issue was trumped by the three other children who still called me Mom, including Jacob, then three years old. I became accustomed to dragging him with me to the girls' back-to-school nights and sporting events. Like most preschool-aged children, his demands were high. At one of Jessica's track meets, in a hurry as usual, I rushed to get to the starting line to see her race. I was almost there when he pulled and tugged at my hand so insistently that he almost knocked me over. Out of frustration, I turned and shouted, "What? Jacob! What do you want?"

"I want to see my brudder."

"What do you mean?" I asked, leaning closer.

"I want to see my brudder," he said, pointing to the press box at the top of the stadium.

"Jacob. What do you mean?" I said again, squatting to his level.

"I want to see JD," he said, pointing and pulling me toward the press box.

I stood and looked up, stared at the press box, and then at Jacob. "I don't see him."

"Right there," he said. "Hims right there." He pointed firmly toward the skybox.

I stood there in the midst of spectators rushing by, staring. I waited there too stunned to move until Jacob a couple of minutes later said, "Okay, hims gone," took my hand, and started walking. Jacob was like this when he was young. He referred to his "grandpa in space" often in those days and said, "My grandpa in space says this and him says that." It was like he was tuned into a radio channel I could not hear. But this incident at the stadium was beyond anything I had experienced with him before.

Lisa Solis DeLong

A Flicker of Compassion

Three years after Justin died, still adjusting to life without him, I began realizing that when you've had a child with cancer and seem intact enough to get out of bed in the morning, brush your teeth, and function, people come to you for advice. Like it or not, I had become an expert on everything from where to go for treatment to what to give a mother, brother, sister, father, or friend when they were diagnosed.

I didn't like this, and at first it annoyed me. I was through with cancer. Justin's battle was lost, and I was not the victor. I was only interested in taking care of my family and did not want to involve myself in anything else. But people called or bumped into me at the market or the park, all with the same question: "So and so was diagnosed with cancer. What should I do?" Eventually I made up my mind not to fight it. A flicker of compassion began to arise, and I chose to go with the flow, to take the on ramp and drive among the victims of the catastrophe known as cancer. I was afraid I might break down, but something in me pushed to go for it. This is how the Holy Spirit works, like it or not: by nudging and pointing us in a direction we do not want to go. The families who endured the same hardship that I had became tender to me.

I decided to follow this prompt after returning to hospital nursing to work as a mother-baby nurse. I was becoming bored with such lighthearted work because deep down, all I wanted to do was talk about Justin. A hospital nursery is not the most conducive place for sharing about your dead son. One day, a coworker came to me when death came near. A twenty-year-old patient had delivered her first baby prematurely because of complications from metastasized breast cancer.

"I just wanted to warn you that this is a cancer-related case," she said in a concerned voice. "Will you be okay?"

"Thank you for telling me like this," I told the labor and delivery nurse. "I appreciate you giving me a heads-up." I didn't know if I could handle it, but I knew I wanted to try.

In the days that followed, I discovered that this patient and I were neighbors and I didn't even know about her plight. Earlier, this would not have bothered me; too lost in my own grief, I did not have room for anyone else's. I needed the three years I took to grieve, adjust to raising Jacob, and help my daughters and husband as they grieved too. This was the first time I had the desire to reach out to someone else with a child with cancer, and it felt good. Prior to this patient, I wanted to keep to myself. I didn't want to be a part of the cancer club. I could barely handle my own grief, I'd thought; but what I discovered was that healing comes from sharing loss with others. The dark night of grief was beginning to pass, and a little light peaked through in its place.

This young woman taught me not to hide my grief but to engage with the process. I knew it was time to reach out to those who were traveling along the cancer highway right next to me. My heart ached to be near families dealing with pediatric cancers.

At a bereavement meeting I later attended, one of the mothers put it this way. "When it comes to how to handle grieving people, there are the DGI's and the GI's. The Don't Get It's and the Get It's." Most people who have not suffered severe loss say the lamest things: "You can have more children, can't you?" I had the sense that I was becoming a GI.

Working as a mother-baby nurse was becoming tedious, and I could feel change coming. A calling was rising inside of me and a sense of readiness, even to the point of knowing that a job opportunity was coming. It was as if I could hear a voice saying, "Get ready. Your new work is near. Be ready." I felt change in the air.

Lisa Solis DeLong

Risk

My career change happened at a pool party the summer of 2004, two years before Jacob's diagnosis. The MHF was hosting their annual barbeque and swim event, and I attended as I had the two prior years. I never went while Justin was alive. There wasn't enough time or wellness.

The party was held at the expansive home of one of the families who had experienced the challenge of the disease through their son when he battled bone cancer. He was several years past treatment and living a health-filled life, and they were generous and welcoming. The backyard was a child's paradise, complete with swimming pool, hot tub, jungle gym, sandbox, basketball court, and pedal cars for racing.

After the hamburgers and hot dogs, one of the MHF board members asked me to go for a walk. As we walked away from the festivities, she said, "I have something to ask you, but I don't want you to feel obligated to answer right away."

"Okay," I said.

"Would you consider coming to work for the MHF as their family outreach coordinator? It would mean working closely with all of our families, and I know this might be difficult for you since Justin has passed. If it is too much or too soon, I totally understand. But I think you would be really good at this position."

"Let me think about it," I said. I smiled. "Okay. I'd love to take the position."

"What? Seriously, do you want more time to think about it?"

"No," I said. "You want to know something strange? I practically knew this was coming. I just didn't know it would be you or the MHF."

When meeting families struggling with pediatric cancer for the first time, all I had to say was, "My son had leukemia too," and they would spill. I met a boy named David Hatfield this way. He was Jacob's age and had a chronic kind of leukemia. He was one of the first children I visited at home. I was apprehensive. I knew that he endured severe bone pain, but his smile put me at ease. He invited me to see his pet snakes, and we talked about spiders and bugs until he became too tired. He sat close to me, and I felt the strongest urge to touch him, but I didn't want to cause him more pain. He was thin and pale and soft and warm. I sat on the couch in the family room, and he cuddled up to me and fell asleep. His mother said that he hadn't been sleeping much because of the pain. She couldn't believe he fell asleep with me touching him. That was a pivotal moment. I enjoyed feeling a sense of purpose, a calling.

One day, Courtney, the event coordinator at the foundation, came into my office and sat down. I could tell she wanted to talk; but we were working, and I didn't want to get sidetracked. We had a light conversation that I thought should end, but she hovered by the door like a kid waiting at the principal's office.

Finally, she said, "I'm going to see Charles, my psychic, this afternoon." She knew where I stood on the psychic issue and that I wasn't into it.

"Oh, well, if anyone comes through for me, tell them I said hello," I joked.

"Well," she paused, lowering her eyes, "someone did come through for you when I went a few weeks ago. But I know how you feel about the whole psychic thing and I didn't know if I should tell you."

I stopped what I was doing and pushed back from my desk.

"Courtney, tell me about it," I prompted. "What happened?"

She hesitated for a moment. "It was Justin."

My stomach jumped.

"As soon as I sat down for my reading, Charles said, 'Who's Lisa?' I said, 'I work with three women named Lisa,' and he said, 'One of them lost a son to a blood disease of some kind. Tell her if she comes, he'll come.'"

I held my breath, nodded, and didn't know what to say. I couldn't get back to work. All I could think about was meeting this guy, this psychic guy. *How could he know I worked with Courtney anyway? Did he surf the Internet? He'd better not be faking it. What if it really was Justin? What if my rabbit hole dream was right? What if he really was trying to reach me?*

That day before Courtney left, I asked her to ask Charles for confirmation that it was Justin.

"I just need to know it's really him."

I prayed silently all evening. *Please take this away from me if it is not something You want for me. But if it is, please let me know if this man, Charles, this psychic man, loves You.*

The next day, I arrived to work early. As soon as Courtney walked in the door, I asked, "So, how was your visit?"

She said that she'd told Charles about my need for confirmation. According to Courtney, he said, "Justin is showing me something about a golf tournament. He liked golf, and he really appreciated this golf tournament. He wants his mom to know that it was very special to him."

I lifted my hand to cover my mouth.

"Yeah," she said. "And after that, he said the strangest thing. He said, 'Courtney, do you know Jesus?'"

I put my other hand over my mouth. Courtney continued.

"I didn't know what to say." Pacing, she continued. "He said, 'He loves you very much and He died for you. Do you know this?' That was so weird. Why would he ask me that?" she said.

I knew exactly why.

When Courtney left my office, I picked up the phone and made the appointment to see her psychic. I did not tell him that I knew Courtney, and I only told him my first name. At least this time I could sin without a national audience.

A week later, three years after Randy first told me about Justin coming through, I drove to a seer's house with Jessica, who, at sixteen, had adjusted well to being the oldest child in our family, in other words, she was good at speaking her mind and bossing us around. She was much bolder than I was at her age. I suppose that is what happens to a little girl after witnessing her brother's death. Jessica knew what she wanted and had no problem conveying it. She had already heard all the stories about her cousin Randy's *Beyond* encounter, as it was relayed to the entire family. She had told me that if I ever went to a psychic without her, she would not forgive me. Her wrath was the last thing I wanted. If Justin was coming through, she was going to be there.

"You can come with me," I said, "but if it gets too weird, you have to wait in the car. And if you're traumatized for life and need psychotherapy when you grow up, you have to promise to eventually forgive me."

We laughed. She agreed.

We were silent with excitement, like two girls cutting class. We pulled up to a sparsely landscaped, tan, stucco house just a few blocks up from the home of a close friend of mine. I parked across the street and two houses up. *No sense sharing our little secret with anyone else,* I thought. The front yard was barren of lawn but not entirely without vegetation, a desert look. The house was a compact, single-story that looked like a modern-day version of a gingerbread house with nothing but Red Hots trimming the upper edge.

Jessica and I held hands and rang the doorbell. Through the one-way screen came a gentle voice. "Just a minute."

Unable to see him through the door; the confessionals of the Catholic church I attended in childhood surfaced in my memory. I didn't like needing a priest to intercede for me when I was young, and I didn't like needing a psychic to intercede for me now; but the desire of my heart to find out anything I could about Justin outweighed the logic of my theology, and I stood there, waiting for the door to open.

"Hi. I'm Charles. Come on in."

He was much shorter and less toned than I had envisioned from his business card photo, where he looked more like a GI Joe rather than the pudgy, unimposing man in front of me. He gestured for us to come in. We sat at a simple wooden dining table in the kitchen.

"Are you here for a reading or trying to contact someone?" he asked.

"I'm not sure," I said as he opened a carved, wooden box about the size of one used to hold recipes and pulled out a stack of Tarot cards. I wrinkled my nose and indicated that I wasn't comfortable with those. He explained that he wasn't comfortable with them at first either.

He said he was raised in a Christian home and struggled with his abilities in early adulthood. He said, "Angels speak to me. That is how I know what I know, how I make contact with people on the other side."

He explained to me that at one point in his life, he had gotten so tired of hearing angels that he prayed to have this ability taken away. One day at church, while sitting among the congregation, a visiting evangelist was preaching. And in the middle of his sermon, he stopped, pointed at him, and said, "You have a gift, and you need to use it!"

Charles said, "I have used it ever since. I didn't like the cards either, but I met another Christian woman who taught me how to use them and told me not to be afraid of them. I keep a photo of her right here. See?" He held a photo of a benign-looking elderly woman with a sincere smile. "The cards just help me communicate, stay organized."

I felt weepy all of a sudden. I couldn't tell if I was crying because I had stooped so low or because I was relieved to finally be there.

He shuffled the cards. He paused and tilted his head as if listening to someone in another room. "Do you have a Catholic background?" he asked, placing the stack of cards in front of him on the table.

"Yes. I was raised Catholic."

"Who is Rose?'

"I don't know anyone named Rose," I replied.

"Did your mother lose a baby? He was only a couple of days old?"

"Yes. My mother's second child, my brother, Joseph, died years before I was born."

Picking up the cards again, keeping them closed in his hands, he said, "Someone is coming through, a very old woman. She has passed recently and is holding her heart."

"My grandmother, Victoria Solis, died recently. She was a hundred and three years old."

"Yes. That's it." He put the cards down. "There's a man here." He paused again. "He died from a blood disease."

"My son died from leukemia."

"Okay. This makes sense. Yes. It is your son. He's here. He is standing right behind you."

Jessica and I looked over my shoulder in the direction he was pointing and saw nothing but the faded kitchen cupboards.

He pushed the cards aside. "When someone comes through like this, they get priority. There are a lot of angels here too. Are you a Christian?"

"Yes," I said.

He proceeded to talk to Jessica and me.

He looked at Jessica. "You have a sister?"

"Yes," she replied.

"Her birthday is next month, in August?"

"Yes."

"He wants you to know he will be there for her party."

Jessica lowered her eyes.

He paused, listened, and then chuckled. "Don't worry, Jessica. He remembers your birthday too. It's near the first of the year, in January, right? He'll be there for your birthday too."

Jessica began to cry. We listened as he described what he was hearing.

"You have a little brother too."

We nodded.

"He says he is around him often."

This made sense to me, and I nodded in agreement.

"He says heaven is wonderful. He teaches children to golf. You know when someone comes to earth as a prodigy, it's because they have been practicing in heaven. He says his favorite part about being there is that he gets to visit with Jesus. He says that Jesus comes and teaches people in groups. He tells stories like he did when he was here on earth like those described in the Bible, 'Only now I under-stand them,' he says."

I cried.

After an hour of translating for us, Charles asked if we had any questions for Justin because we were running out of time. He grabbed a tissue and wiped the tears from his eyes, emotional, he said, from the love Justin was conveying through him.

"He's a really good man," the psychic said, "a very, very good man. And he just keeps pouring out pink roses. That is how people on the other side symbolize love."

He said to ask Justin questions directly in our minds, to talk to him and he would receive Justin's answer and tell us. In my mind, I asked Justin about the rabbit-hole dream. Was it him trying to reach me?

A few seconds later, without my ever mentioning the dream out loud, Charles nodded. "Justin visited you in a dream? Okay. It was him, but not because he needed anything from you. He wants you to know this. He doesn't need you. He was so excited about heaven, what it is like, that he wanted you to see it. He wanted to share it with you. That's all."

Again, I cried.

Jessica and I left the psychic's house, hugging and laughing and making fun of ourselves.

"Wow, Mom. That was so weird. But you know what. I feel better, kind of lighter."

"Me too," I said.

We got in to the car and drove home.

"Can you believe he knew all that stuff about our birthdays and how upset I was that Justin remembered Jojo's birthday and not mine?"

"I know. That was so strange, wasn't it? What about knowing that Nana lost a baby? No one knows that stuff."

"Mom, do you believe him?"

"I think I do, Jess. He was so likeable. His eyes were kind. And the way he cried. And he was so right-on about so many things. I'll have to think about this for a while. All I know right now is I'm awfully glad you came with me. If I told anyone about this, they wouldn't believe me."

"I'm glad I came too, Mom."

"Please don't tell anyone for a while. I don't want to have to explain myself to anyone. It's too hard. Besides, no one will believe it anyway."

"I know what you mean. Don't worry, Mom. I won't tell anyone about it until you do."

"Okay. Thanks, Jess. I love you."

"I love you too, Mom."

For weeks after the psychic experience, I didn't talk to anyone about what had happened. I was afraid that I was being a poor example of what a faithful Christian was supposed to be. I needed time to let the experience soak in before anyone could beat it down. I read *One Last Time* by John Edwards in an attempt at gaining some perspective. I hid the cover so no one would know what I was reading. I didn't want anyone's input or opinion. I was conditioned to believe that even reading a book by a person in his field was risky. What I learned was that he was just a man with a unique life experience that I could relate to.

The death of a child is the closest encounter a human being can have to dying themselves—a "near death experience" of another kind. Not having a penchant for wandering in soul-less restlessness, I read *The Case for Christ* by Lee Strobel. In it he described the process Jesus's body went through in the hours leading to his death. Coming from a Catholic background in my childhood and a Four Square, Evengelical Free, and Baptist combo-pack experience as an adult, I had heard all about Christ's life, suffering, and death to the point, I was ashamed to say, of boredom. But in the quagmire of deep loss, death mattered to me—now it was personal.

When I read the forensic evidence in Strobel's book, the depictions of what Christ endured and how His body would have succumbed to severe dehydration, lack of oxygen, and ultimately heart failure; the graphic images of Justin's passing mirrored Christ's, in a way that touched me. The cause of death as it read on Justin's Death Certificate—"Heart Failure"—would likely have been written on Christ's own certificate of death had He existed in modern times. It always struck me as odd that there was nothing about Justin's cancer on his death certificate. I supposed there wasn't enough room for the entirety of what leads to a person's death on one piece of paper. For some, that would take a book.

Strobel's imagery brought Christ's dead body to my front door, right on top of Justin's.

As the weeks passed, I had to make sense of the psychic experience. As I replayed it in my mind, I felt annoyed that I didn't know who Rose was. I asked my brother, Ken, one day if he knew of anyone in our family named Rose.

"Yeah," he said without hesitating. "Grandma Solis had a sister named Rose. They called her Mother Rose because she was a nun."

"Really?" I asked, stunned.

"Yeah. Don't you remember? Grandma always wanted to be a nun like her but decided to get married instead. You never heard that story before?"

I had no recollection of this bit of family history; but Ken, being five years older than me, always seemed to know more about our grandparents. I felt relieved that Rose was real. It meant that the psychic's abilities were real too.

I thought about all the Bible stories that I didn't fully understand. Some of them were weird and inesplicable by today's standards, and some were so powerful they had changed my life forever. I recalled the story of Balaam being stopped by his donkey on a dusty road, Balaam beating the donkey until the animal turned to him in disgust and spoke, admonishing him for ignoring God's instructions. Afterward, Balaam was a changed man. I wondered how he must have felt when he told people his story, knowing full well they would not believe that his donkey actually uttered words.

I came to the conclusion that if God could make a jackass speak, He could certainly empower a man to hear angels.

After meeting with Charles, I began to feel better, joyful, liberated. That tugging feeling I'd had prompting me to make sense of the rabbit-hole dream was gone. I began talking to Justin more and included my grandmother and her sister, silent, heartfelt conversations where I might not have heard their responses, but I felt somehow connected. My Catholic roots began to make sense to me in a way I never quite appreciated until the image of my grandmother standing beside me brought my religious life full circle. My prayers changed from pleading requests to peaceful recognitions. I found myself saying, "Thank you, Jesus," for this and, "Thank you, Jesus," for that. Seeing a spiritual advisor was not something I felt proud of at the time; but after reflecting on the outcome of the experience, I'm glad I went. If I had let fear dominate and not gone, I wouldn't have the images of heaven I needed. It was not the argument of theologians that had solved the problems of my questioning heart but the certainty that I had been heard.

After a few months of keeping the incident to myself, while Dave and I were on vacation, I told him about it. He listened and responded with much less reprehension than I had thought he would. He cried when I told him about Justin golfing. He didn't like that I went, but he understood my need to explore the opportunity. He even admitted to feeling a little jealous.

"Jealous of what?" I asked.

"I don't know exactly. Maybe that you felt close or that he talked to you. I don't know."

I only shared the Charles incident with my sisters and closest friends at first. I'm sure they thought I was going off the deep end of a spiritually glacial crevice; but once they knew the details, their concern for me turned to a shared peace in their grieving for Justin too.

Once I felt more secure with the consequences of having seen a psychic—that my head did not spin and my faith not only remained but grew—I began sharing my experience with families in grief support group. When I did, I discovered that many parents had gone to spiritual advisors, but they hadn't shared their experiences with anybody because they were afraid of appearing foolish. The isolation one feels after the loss of a child can lead to paralyzing depression, as it did with a friend of mine who committed suicide after the loss of his son. There was risk involved in sharing the telepathic aspect of my experience, but if doing so eased the despair of even one grief-stricken parent, then it was worth taking.

I've wanted to run back to Charles many times since, simply wanting to know the future during extreme stress. But just like when I was young and didn't like relying on a priest, I found that I didn't like thinking that I had to rely on Charles. He never pressured me to visit him again and encouraged my own spiritual growth and independence. That was the trademark of someone I could trust.

In the months that followed, when the teachings of priests and pastors echoed in my mind and I felt small and afraid like I did as a child, I found the ability to continue to search the life of Christ to help me understand. In doing so, I came to feel less crazy and more comforted by the images I was given of Justin functioning, existing with other people, spending time with the one I still called Lord, in a place I recognized. I found a way to let my mind voyage into a future that included him.

Most nights after, when I nestled into my bed with the longing to see my firstborn son, I found myself talking to two gray-haired women: my grandmother, Victoria, and her sister, Rose. I imagined them wearing simple shifts, each one carrying a rosary in her pocket, walking slowly arm in arm. Laying on my back stretching, I'd place my hands under my head and then speak silently to Justin. I could picture him sitting with a group of friends, listening to the Master teacher, maybe having a cool drink after a game of golf. As his day came to an end, I could almost see him pause to rest and lay his head on his pillow. In those moments, I embraced the possibility that he might visit his mother in a dream.

The Mercy Seat

Journal entry 6/5/2006

A blank page, how challenging. After a day like today, I am
spent, wasted beyond myself.

Jacob has had a cough. He has had a cough and low-grade
fever for eight days. He has had a cough, a low-grade fever, and bleeding gums. This morning, swollen, puffy, dark
circled eyes. Blood work has revealed he is slightly anemic, 9
something Hgb, elevated white cells, not extremely elevated,
just elevated, and blah la blah la blah. I can't think. I don't
remember lab values anymore. I only remember having gone
through this before and how pissed I am at the thought of the
possibility of going through it again.

Mercy seats, also known as misericords, are obscured treasures of
medieval cathedrals, abbey churches, and some parish churches all
over Europe. The first time I saw one was when Jacob and I visited
Hearst Castle. The mercy seat is a small ledge underneath a choir
seat that can be leaned on when it is tipped up, helping monks stand

for long periods, a sort of leaning butt shelf. The area beneath the ledge often has carvings, sometimes with religious themes but more often with charming, humorous, and even vulgar scenes of medieval life like the one showing a drunken man being beaten by his wife. Many misericords are anti-feminist, showing women with hideous grins or as devils, which makes me wonder if the beaten husband was the craftsmen. Scenes vary depending on the church. Some are of mythical creatures and pigs dancing to bagpipe music, while others poke fun at the shape of the buttocks. My favorite discovery related to the mercy seat are the carvings of popular thirteenth-century proverbs that can be found underneath the location of where the rear would sit:

"Money is useful but not worth anything in the face of death."
"Sail when the wind allows."
"Don't pull too hard on a weak rope."

It was Monday June 5, 2006, Dave was at home with Jacob, and I was at the Michael Hoefflin Foundation's Family Fun Night at Mountasia. It was no place for quiet as the ding, ding, ding of the pinball games; bright, flashing lights; and screams of delight marked our sixth year of dark knowledge, the kind that came after Justin's death, with discovering that fun events for kids with cancer existed even after they were gone. This was my second year of employment by the Foundation. I had come to view these events as my place of worship among fellow parishioners. Kids squealed at the sight of tickets pouring out of slots from games they were playing, knowing this meant they would have greater options at the redemption counter later. A boy ran by with a long stream of paper tickets coiled into a wad in his hands as he lunged toward the prizes.

"I'll take the glow-in-the-dark rocket!" he shouted.

These kids looked like any other—at least most of them did: full heads of hair, tennis shoes, T-shirts with Mario Bros. or Volcom logos on them. But looking closer, there were those who were different. Like the hidden scenes below mercy seats of old, they were there; but you had to look for them, or you'd miss them. They were the ones with pale skin and bald heads under baseball caps. Their eyebrows, or rather lack thereof, gave them away.

Mountasia was the perfect place for the annual Family Arcade night, where parents, patients, and siblings could come play games, ride go-carts, or fire squirt guns from bumper boats and enjoy pizza and ice cream, all for free. Being the family outreach coordinator for the Foundation was a way for me to fulfill my calling. It held me up. Since Justin's passing, I needed to be among families like mine. This was where I found comfort. This particular event was one of my favorites. I loved meeting families under such upbeat circumstances, away from hospital beds, IV monitors, and needle pokes. Tonight was all about fun. The work was what I leaned on, the seat that gave my legs strength to endure the long worship service I considered my life.

I saw families I knew, the Hills and Holzers, the Torps and Tuluengas—families with children who had cancer and were being treated; families who had children who were well, their cancer beaten; and families, like mine, who brought surviving siblings adjusting to life without the brother or sister who died.

In a couple of weeks, kindergarten would be over and the summer fun would begin. I looked forward to beach trips, swimming pools, and our annual trip to Mammoth Mountain to hike rugged trails and smell pine-scented air during summer thunderstorms. But this evening was about families living with childhood cancers. I mingled and smiled and handed out blue bracelets to identify who was part of our group and who was not. I met three new families who had come to this MHF event for the first time. They were a bit dazed, and they smiled a half grin, a sort of wince, as I greeted them. I understood their misgivings. I had not wanted to be a part of this club either.

I walked over to the bumper boats. From there I could see Jojo riding the go-carts, her favorite attraction. She was smiling as she turned the steering wheel hard and her hair blew steady in the wind. She had come with me that evening. She wouldn't have missed it. Jacob had not been feeling well the past few days. I had taken him to the doctor on Friday because a little cough he'd been fighting all week had lingered. That and a low-grade fever had been enough for me to decide to have him examined.

"Bring him back on Monday if he has not improved," Dr. Tang said, and I agreed.

That morning, he was still coughing and running a low-grade fever, and his gums were bleeding when he brushed his teeth. I returned to Dr. Tang's office as instructed and insisted on checking his blood. I needed peace of mind. Jacob had many colds this year, his first year of public school; but this year of sniffles and sneezes was almost over. And soon we would be building sandcastles on the beach. I was standing, leaning on the evidence of six years of having two healthy daughters and a son, buoyed by a life that was full and enjoyable and, most of the time, beyond grief.

At the bumper boats, I saw three men standing by the fence; and I knew them from the grief support group, Hope Hereafter. One was leaning against the fence. The others swayed back and forth in a sort of solemn dance, looking down at their feet, no doubt talking about how hard it was to be there without their beautiful child. Like me, I imagined they were thinking, *All the games in the world can't make me smile right now, but look at his brother or her sister as they squirt water and bump in the boats. Look at their smile and laughter. Her brother used to love it here too, at the arcade, before the leukemia or the bone cancer or the brain tumor.* I felt their pain. They had a look I knew too well, and I was glad they found each other there among the gaiety.

My cell phone rang, and I made the mistake of answering it.

"Hello, Dave. Is that you? It's noisy here. Can you talk louder?"

"Lees, the doctor called!" he shouted.

He had that tone in his voice, the one I'd heard before; but it had been so long that I didn't figure it out at first. I thought he was upset about his mother, who had been ill.

"What do you mean? Which doctor?" I walked toward the front of the building, looking for quiet. I pressed the phone hard to my ear and smiled as a family wearing the blue bracelets walked by.

"It's Jacob. His doctor called."

I heard him and kept walking toward the exit.

"Lees, they want us to bring him to Childrens Hospital tomorrow for a bone marrow test. His blood tests are not right. I'm sorry to tell you this, but they think he might have leukemia."

I opened the front glass double doors and felt the heat of the evening sun. Its piercing rays hurt my eyes, and I raised my free hand to shade my face.

"What do you mean? What did she say? What was his white cell count? Were there blast cells?"

I heard myself ask these questions but couldn't believe it was me asking them. I had not had thoughts like that in six years. I didn't think I remembered lab values, but the words come out.

"A bone marrow test? They want to do a bone marrow aspiration? On Jacob? How can this be? This must be a mistake."

"I thought the same thing, Lees, but I asked everything I could. It is not a mistake. We have to bring him in tomorrow."

I dropped my arms to my side after hanging up and walked over to a patch of grass near the entrance, where my legs collapsed beneath me like a folding chair. I was flattened.

I was no longer leaning on the mercy seat.

I sat on the cool, scratchy grass, holding my head in my hands, and the tears came. I didn't know what to do. I was among my people, but the intense dread I felt was crippling. I couldn't do this again—battle my child's cancer. Should I go back inside and tell them Jacob might have leukemia? I couldn't say it, here and now, in the midst of air hockey and skee-ball, it didn't seem feasible.

I continued to sit on the grass, and then I looked up at the sky. There was a small airplane buzzing by with white smoke pouring from its tail end. Like white chalk on a blue chalkboard, I watched it curve and dip as 6 6 6 was drawn across the sky. Tears streamed down my face. The next day was June 6, 2006. *What the hell was this?* I thought. *Why was someone up in a plane writing that? Why was I here looking at it?* I felt nauseous. In a few minutes, my friend Candye walked toward me from the parking lot, just arriving for the festivities.

She was hurried and eager to get to the party; but when she saw me, she stopped and asked, "What's wrong? What happened?"

She sat down on the grass with me, and I told her what Dave had just told me.

I began to grasp it as I said it out loud to her. "He might have leukemia."

I told her that I didn't know what to do, and she sat with me until I was ready to stand. I walked back inside and told the Hoefflins why I had to leave. They were shocked and offered to drive Jojo home for me. Candye promised to take care of her too. I didn't want to ruin her fun, not now, not ever. She was enjoying herself, which wasn't a problem for her in this setting among other siblings who's brother or sister had died too. I thought about Jessica, who, at seventeen, preferred to avoid cancer-related family events. *She remembered more of the horrors of leukemia than Jojo* I thought; and my heart hurt to think about the girls and what tomorrow would bring.

I drove the fifteen minutes home as popcorn memories exploded in my mind—Dr. V's voice in 1990, nurse Kathy's smile when we left CHLA in 1995, wondering if anyone we knew would still be there. I looked at Jacob as soon as I opened the front door. He was lying on the couch, his head on Dave's lap. Dave was stroking his hair, when they looked at me. Dave and I began to tear up. I felt mad at him for telling me such terrible news in the middle of my obligations at the party, for not protecting me at least until my time of joyful service was over; but I softened when I saw the hurt in his eyes.

When Jojo came home an hour later she asked, "Why did you leave, Mom? Is Jacob okay?"

This question would be asked too many times for one young life. We told the girls what was happening when they both got home. They were shocked and quiet. Dave and I went to bed with Jacob sleeping between us. All he knew was that he had to see the doctor the next day. The thought of it was not going all the way in. I could only grasp the idea in stabs of pain that lead to outbursts of weeping.

We drove to Childrens Hospital the same way we drove when it was Justin in the backseat. Dave and I were silent. I looked back at Jacob and had to remind myself what year this was. He looked so much like Justin at this age. Even he was fooled when I showed him a photo of Justin, and he thought it was him. But it was not Justin now. It was Jacob. It felt the same, the panic, the anxiety, the helplessness, the desire to run away.

We pulled up to the front of CHLA, where a parking attendant took our car. Valet parking and no McDonald's. Things had changed. The front of the hospital had been updated with a new, modern foyer where natural light poured in through two-story, high windows and a colorful mural depicted Los Angeles city life. Its blue hue flowed along the top of the entry like a banner fluttering in a parade. People walked past desks where clerks asked where we were going and gave us bright orange stickers that "must be worn at all times." These were our tickets to the theme park known as Hematology/Oncology Outpatient. I said it like that now; but soon, it would be "Hem/Onc." That was how the locals said it.

Dave and I walked with Jacob between us, past the coffee kiosk where frappuccinos were blending and lattes were steaming. The aroma of coffee was enticing, but I reminded myself that this was not the time for frivolous drinks; and we kept walking down the corridor, past the elevator, across the bridge over DeLongpre Street, and up the outpatient tower to the fifth floor. This tower did not exist when we brought Justin here for the first time. We left CHLA shortly after it opened and only came here a few times before switching to City of Hope. When we stepped off the elevator, the clinic looked smaller than I remembered. We followed the signs to check in. I looked for familiar faces as though no time had passed, but it had been eleven years since the days I last walked those narrow halls with Justin. I was there with my second son. I had to keep reminding myself. *Surely no one will remember us. It has been too long.* I said his name to the clerk and almost started crying. We waited, which was what we would do a lot of in the days, weeks, months, and years to come.

After checking in, which I had forgotten how to do, and fumbling through my purse for insurance cards and phone numbers, we went to triage so Jacob could be weighed. This and his temperature, blood pressure, and pulse were recorded. Then he was tagged with a white, plastic bracelet *Jacob DeLong* and his date of birth. The clerks and technicians were kind and efficient, but I didn't want to be there. I didn't trust them yet. I walked into the triage room with Jacob and slipped his red Crocs off of his feet. He weighed forty-two pounds and was forty inches tall. His temperature was 37.6 °C. I couldn't remember how to convert this, so I asked the nurse.

"It is ninety-nine point seven degrees Fahrenheit," she said, looking at a conversion chart.

It was the same as it had been all week; low enough to lull me in to thinking it was *just another cold* but high enough to make me feel foolish. I'd done it again—not seen it.

Blood was drawn from Jacob's kindergarten-sized arm.

"This is going to hurt, like a pinch," I told him.

It did, and he cried. We waited in the waiting room, Jacob took turns in our arms, until we were called in to the exam room. Jacob sat on the child-sized exam table and drew on the substantial white board strategically placed for easy access. He used red and blue dry erase markers and made broad swirls and dashes in a carefree, artful manner. He loved to draw, and the scale of this canvas was freeing. A familiar face walked through the door: Karla—the social worker with whom I had worked to distribute hospital care kits from the MHF—stepped inside. I helped design the kits for parents of newly diagnosed children who received the shocking news that their child had cancer and were unprepared to stay in the hospital. The kits were filled with items to ease the blow: a blanket and plush stuffed animal for the child, toiletries for the caregiver. Karla came in and gave me a hug.

"What happened?" she asked. "You were just here, delivering kits. I can't believe this."

"I know," I said. "I can't either."

Dave and Karla and Jacob and I sat in the room and waited. A doctor walked in.

"I'm Dr. Glkdjskn," was what it sounded like to me. "It looks like leukemia."

He blurted it out like it was chicken pox or tendonitis. Having to hear it once was bad enough, but the second time it was impossible to hear without coming apart. That is what I did. A plaintiff wail came out from my mouth in such a way that I did not recognize it as mine.

"No, no, no. It can't be leukemia. Not again," I said.

Dave turned toward the wall, faced it, raised his arm, and leaned his head against it. The doctor rolled his eyes and looked away as if my outburst was unacceptable. Jacob pulled hard at his identification bracelet and tried without success to rip it off.

He yelled, "You people are in big trouble! I'm calling nine nine one so the police can come arrest you." He confused the title but not the meaning.

I felt terrible that my outburst had frightened him. I was appalled that the news had come like this. Hadn't anyone told this doctor that it was our second time? Didn't anyone communicate the irrational nature of what we were living? If he'd expected stoicism, he had opened the wrong door.

We asked questions and wanted answers. A bone marrow aspiration and lumbar puncture were scheduled in order to examine

Jacob's marrow cells and spinal fluid for leukemia cells. He was only six years old and knew nothing about the illness that took his brother's life; but I remembered. We would be there for days, and I hadn't packed anything. I had not believed this could happen.

Karla asked, "Do you want me to bring you one of your care kits?"

"Yes," I said, shaking my head and shrugging my shoulders.

Karla left and returned quickly with a blue duffle bag with a white MHF logo on it. The same bags I picked out at wholesale prices in downtown LA with the logo I helped choose and the leopard-print blanket and soft teddy bear I put inside. Jacob pulled out the blanket and wrapped it around himself and then ripped into everything inside; the toothpaste and toothbrush, crayons, and coloring book. He smiled as though it were Christmas. The kit was a big hit just as I had designed it to be. I just never imagined *I* would be the one in need of it.

Jacob was admitted to Four East oncology, where it was confirmed that acute lymphoblastic leukemia (ALL) was the official diagnosis again. The bone marrow aspiration was done under anesthesia. I knew these things were done—that a needle was pressed through Jacob's hip bone and marrow was sucked out and that while he slept, a spinal needle the length of a pen was inserted into his back to extract spinal fluid in search of vagrant leukemia cells—but I couldn't engage. I couldn't remember what I did or where I was during that time. Did I wait in the same waiting room as I had with Justin? Was that the day I went down to the cafeteria where I discovered the new coffee kiosk? Many things had changed at CHLA, but the horror I felt at having a kid there had not.

When Jacob came back to his room with IVs in both hands, he looked like a puppet dangling from two strings. Two lines were needed to keep up with all the blood transfusions and medications. Jacob was not as cooperative about painful procedures as Justin had been at this age. I was glad that he was asleep when this new IV had been started. He was fully awake and was sitting up, drawing pictures; but the IV's were cumbersome as he reached for a falling crayon.

"Ouch," he said as he rearranged the tubing and continued creating.

A couple of days passed, and a different IV was started, a PICC line, a peripherally inserted central catheter, thus its acronym. It was a long, slender, small, flexible tube that was inserted into a peripheral vein where Jacob's left arm bent. As it was inserted, it was advanced until the catheter tip terminated in a large vein in his chest, near his heart. This line was much heftier than a standard IV. The good news was that the IV lines in his hands had been removed, but now Jacob held his arm folded at the elbow as though wearing a sling.

"Open your arm, Jacob. It's okay. You won't hurt it."

"It feels weird. I'll just keep it like this." This is where Justin would have complied. Not so with Jacob. While I was frustrated with his stubbornness, I was at once hopeful that perhaps his feisty nature would help him fight his leukemia in a way that his brother could not.

Stuart Siegel, M.D., associate director for pediatric oncology at USC/Norris, head of the division of hematology-oncology and founding director of the Childrens Center for Cancer and Blood Diseases at Childrens Hospital Los Angeles was assigned as Jacob's doctor. He had been at CHLA for thirty years and replaced Dr. Glskjsn at our request. He was also professor and vice chair of pediatrics at the Keck School of Medicine of USC. I met Dr. Siegel a few months prior at a luncheon hosted by the MHF. He was the presenting speaker. There is intelligent, and then there is super intelligent. Dr. Siegel is the latter.

He was the best, but I was not pleased. I wanted better than the best.

I didn't want a doctor who would not be here when I needed him, and "heads" are not known for their availability.

Dr. Siegel sat down with Dave and me with his team, and we discussed the treatment plan. The plan was laid, but there was "just one problem we need to discuss," I said with an authority I found surprising. "I want Dr. So and So to be Jacob's doctor."

"Why is that?" Dr. Siegel asked, his head tilted, elbow on the table.

"Because I am not new at this, and I know how it is for physicians in your position. You will be gone a lot, and I need someone who will be here when I need them. I can't handle being pawned off to a stranger. I can't handle hoards of new doctors and having to repeat Jacob's case history over and over again. His case is different. We are different, and we need to be treated differently," I said.

"I understand your concern," he said in a calm voice, one eyebrow raised. "I assure you I am available to you, and I am very dependable even when I am out of town. I am in constant contact with my patients, even if I am on an airplane or out of the country. Believe me. I will be here for you." Looking at me directly in the eyes with a kind of paternal authority, he said, "Jacob is *my* patient."

I was like a panicked guard dog, unwilling to receive strangers into my yard. My pup was behind me, and I had to defend him. Pulling out a bag full of supplements, I growled, "Then this is how it is going to be. I am going to give Jacob supplements. I know this was frowned upon when Justin was sick, but I am going to do it this time. And you can either know about it or not."

Again calm, he said, "That's fine. You can give him supplements, but please do me a favor and let me look at them first just to make sure there's nothing in the products that can hurt him."

I handed him the bag, and he reached into his pocket and pulled out a book the size of a thick Bible. He began looking at the ingredients on the bottle labels and then read about each ingredient and its known effect on the body.

"This one can affect him negatively. Everything else is okay," he said with an obvious understanding of the new age of supplementation and cancer therapies.

I began softening at his willingness to concede the supplement issue so quickly. In reality, the thought of giving Jacob herbs, vitamins, and antioxidants scared me, but I felt like I had to do something. Had I learned nothing from his brother? I had to force the issue right from the start. Dave liked Dr. Siegel, and we decided to give the guy a chance. He exuded confidence under fire, and he was calm and caring. He didn't seem intimidated by the prospect of taking on such a high stake case, and that impressed me. I would need that kind of poise in the months to come.

Chemotherapy was given, and blood was drawn to count leukemia cells; and this cycle continued for two weeks. People brought toys, and Jacob thought that was great.

He asked, "What did you bring me?" whenever a visitor stopped in.

My friend Diane ran down to the gift shop and bought him a Godzilla figurine after she showed up empty handed. Jacob was a fast learner; but he didn't know what I knew—that this was just the beginning and it would be hard, that all the toys in the world wouldn't make him well. But, as with Justin, toys put a smile on his face, and that was what he needed. Unlike Justin, Jacob loved to build things; and even though he could be fidgety at times, putting together a new Playmobile set, where he had to open bags of individually wrapped plastic pieces the size of rice and snap them together to create a zoo or a castle, and he could be entertained for hours. Play-Doh was another favorite. He could create an entire video game scene from Mario Brothers, complete with sound effects, on the over-bed table. His scenes included recognizable characters like Luigi and Princess Peach. It was starting to become apparent that Jacob was an artist. He sculpted dinosaurs one day and when the nurse walked in she was able to identify a T-Rex, a Pterodactyl, and a Stegasaurus. I was thankful that pleasing him was so simple.

Justin had not been as creative. He became frustrated with building things like Lego sets. When he was about six years old he built a Playmobile castle set in his bedroom and didn't take it down for weeks. He had followed the instructions step by step and didn't want to have to do it again. Jacob enjoyed assembling as much as tearing down and rarely followed the prescribed directions. It was clear that both boys were very different, but what about their cancers? Like children, leukemia has a personality of its own.

I was told that slides of Justin's blood had been found in the archives of the Childrens Hospital research department. That was what remained of Justin: dried blood smeared on glass; that and his primary teeth, the ones he had left under his pillow for the tooth fairy when he was Jacob's age. I wondered if someday in the distant future scientists would be able to create human beings from such minuscule remnants of DNA. If so, I would be the first to sign up.

Researchers studied my sons under microscopes, comparing Justin's leukemia cells to Jacob's. This was the closest my boys had been in six years: on glass slides, side by side. Justin's cells were shaped like crescent moons, while Jacob's were perfect circles. There were chromosome studies and cytology studies. Their leukemias, like brothers, shared the same name but had different personalities. I thought about asking if I could take a look but decided against it. It wouldn't bring Justin back and I couldn't bring myself to go there, the sight of both boys' names on cold glass. It was discovered that Jacob's cells, the round ones, were easier to treat. Round was better than not. This news gave me hope that at their essence the boys' cancers were as unique as they were and would be the key to Jacob's survival.

Breaking down Jacob's leukemia cells, which was what the chemotherapy began to do, started causing him pain. He had muscle aches and a headache, and he'd had to take so much medication that I didn't want to force him to swallow any more. I rubbed his feet with a blend of essential oils that another mom had given to me. Her daughter, Sophia, had died from leukemia the year before, and we'd met at support group.

"I made this one specifically for Jacob," she told me. "I asked Sophia's angels to help me choose the perfect oils, and I thought it would comfort Jacob."

I was hesitant but willing to give it a try. I'd seen enough by now to know that what works might not come in traditional form. There was no such thing as one-size-fits-all medicine; so rather than give Jacob more toxic chemicals, I took out the oil and rubbed it on my hands. The scent of the oil was soothing, like being in a meadow after it rained. As I rubbed it on Jacob's soft, little feet, I prayed to Jesus to help relieve his discomfort. I found myself doing this more and more. Who else was there to turn to in a lonely hospital room where kids whimpered and mothers wept? In a few minutes, he stopped moaning and began breathing deeply, falling in to a restful sleep. I was amazed, exhausted and suddenly relaxed. I fell asleep curled up at his feet.

After two weeks of being hospitalized, Jacob was discharged to a three-year sentence of outpatient chemotherapy and blood tests.

I was relieved to be going home, unlike other parents—the ones I'd seen in the hallways on Four East late at night—like the Hatfields, familiar faces from my recent past. David was there fighting his leukemia too. I remembered visiting them at home and another day when little David and Jacob had gone on a nature hike together, which I had organized while acting as the family outreach coordinator. We'd had an adventurous day studying stick bugs and giant cockroaches which both boys held and examined with healthy enthusiasm. There in the hospital they were faced with the bleak truth that David's leukemia was not likely to go away, and I was faced with having a child with cancer again. I felt lousy leaving them there.

Jacob's treatments were scheduled and would require driving thirty miles to CHLA from Santa Clarita every day at first. The phases of treatment had not changed from when Justin had received them: induction, consolidation, interim maintenance, delayed intensification. Each phase involved a different series of chemotherapy drugs: L-asparaginase, vincristine, and a steroid called dexamethasone. Other drugs would be added later: methotrexate and 6-mercaptopurine; the list went on. These were the same drugs that were used on Justin both times, except for the steroid. He had been on Prednisone. Dexamethasone, aka Decadron, was prednisone's meaner big brother.

A month later, after the induction phase, the PICC line was removed and a different central IV line, a portacath, was surgically placed under anesthesia in Jacob's upper clavicular region. Seeing your kid wheeled off on a gurney never gets easy, whether the first time or the fiftieth. Dave and I waited in the same waiting room as we had when Justin first got his Hickman inserted. This time, we entered the recovery room to a bone chilling scream that made the nurses rush to Jacob's side. This went on for thirty minutes. The nurse instructed him not to yell, and when she walked away I whispered in his ear, "Scream as loud as you want, Jacob." I felt strangely proud of my little wild cat.

He could not straighten his left arm, where the PICC line had been. It was stuck in the bent position like a wire hanger and would take weeks of exercise to release and regain full extension. With the PICC line gone, Jacob was afforded new freedoms. The portacath was designed to permit repeated access to Jacob's venous system for the parenteral delivery of medications, fluids, and for the sampling of venous blood. It left a one-inch scar and a bump the size of a soda cap under Jacob's skin like a little bowl under a rug. It was tender to the touch, and Jacob winced when it was accessed, which was like having a metal mosquito with a stinger the size of a hummingbird's beak poke through the skin in order to reach the saucer of blood just beneath the surface. When it worked, on the first try, it was the greatest IV invention ever created; and when it did not, it was just another irritant I wanted to swat away in the oncology jungle. Still, it afforded Jacob total freedom to swim and bathe and required no maintenance on my part; and that, as Martha Stewart says, was a "good thing."

Six weeks after diagnosis, we were settling in to the life of a cancer patient. Our family and friends were as stunned as we were that this was our life again. There was great suffering in our community as the news of Jacob's diagnosis traveled.

"I felt like I was kicked in the stomach when I found out," was a recurring comment.

The families I'd been working with at the MHF sent kind notes of kindred heartache which lifted my spirits as I felt the disappointment of having resigned from the family outreach position. I was sad to stop working outside of my home, but it was either stop taking care of other people's families or have a nervous breakdown.

"Don't pull too hard on a weak rope."

A fitting statement when it was carved into the bottom of a mercy seat years ago. I heeded the advice and began the task of holding my life together.

Dave's coworkers began rallying the troops. Parents from his cross-country team started brainstorming with folks from all over the Santa Clarita Valley. People from Heart of the Canyons Church, and many friends volunteered to help our ailing family. When I called Jim Etzel in Portland, our hero from the Justin years, he vowed to call upon his people. A friend of his who worked for Vons.com set us up with free groceries delivered to our home. This was one of the most practical gifts anyone could give a family like ours, where the risk of taking Jacob to the grocery store far outwayed the need for food. I had never used a service like this before, but I quickly fell in love with it when the items I ordered online came streaming into my kitchen without me ever having to step foot out of my front door. It also allowed all three kids to shop together. They would go online and shop aisle by aisle picking out everything from barbequed potato chips to Pop-Tarts and then I would edit the list and pile on the organic eggs and soy milk. Vons had the largest selection of organic products I had found at the time and their online shopping made it easy to access them.

The community of Santa Clarita reached out as our friends—the Golds, Broneers, Velardes and Pattersons—formed a committee to organize a charity event on our behalf: The Jakie Jog. I was so consumed with caring for Jacob that I knew little about what was transpiring. I was a bat in a cave, leaving only when necessary.

The Jakie Jog was scheduled for July 23, a week after the sixth anniversary of Justin's death; but there was no room for reminiscing now. Life trumped death. On that anniversary, I spent the day combating a fever in the ER of CHLA, trying to keep Jacob alive.

On the day of the Jakie Jog, I drove in to the parking lot at Canyon High at around noon, where the event was taking place. I had not been sure that Jakie, his pet name, would be able to make it at all. But feverless and eager to join the party, he gathered enough strength to attend. As we got closer, I saw rainbow balloon arches, which led to a field full of people surrounded by inflatable bounce houses, craft booths, dunk tanks, and table after table of food. I heard a live band playing. *All of this is for Jacob, for our family,* I thought and I started to cry. I saw a man in plaid shorts jumping up and down, waving his arms; and I realized that it is my brother-in-law, Mike.

Jojo shouted, "Auntie Cathie's here!"

At that, Jakie unbuckled and was out of his car seat, yelling, "Momo! Coco!"

I saw my little sister and her kids—Mikala, Emily, and Isaiah—all there, and I cried some more. I did not know that they were coming. They had driven all the way from Austin, Texas, to be there for

Blood Brothers

Jacob's walk. I saw the distress on my sister's face when her eyes met Jacob's for the first time since his diagnosis and realized how much his appearance had changed.

Jacob's cousins were good medicine for Jacob. He had outbursts of energy that I hadn't seen in weeks. He was pale and losing some hair, but they didn't seem to notice. All they saw was the cousin they loved, and they embraced Jacob with laughter and helped him down to the track where they frolicked in sprinklers and got soaked in the stifling heat.

It was 116 degrees—a record, but despite the extreme heat, people still walked and jogged around the track. Many of them had walked the same oval when it was Justin's memorial being held there. They walked and talked, while the rock band from Heart of the Canyons Church jammed on electric guitars and keyboards. They played for four hours with sweat dripping off their soaked foreheads. I found comfort in the familiarity of their lead singer, Jim's, smooth raspy tenor. I felt remorse for not attending worship services more often, for not supporting the church more, for bowing out of active participation even though I knew in my state of mourning over the years since Justin passed, it wasn't something I could handle much of. I felt humbled by these folks. This was worship at its best.

I noticed one man running lap after lap in the heat but I didn't recognize him.

"Who is that?" I asked, but no one knew.

Every time I looked up, he was running. I wouldn't find out until a couple of weeks later while looking at the signature board, where visitors autographed and wrote well wishes to Jacob, that the man running with such diligence was Tony Potts of *Access Hollywood*. We had not met, but I felt a sense of kinship after seeing how hard he had worked to make a difference in the life of a child he didn't know. When it comes to childhood cancers, strangers make the most amazing sacrifices.

It seemed like everyone was wearing Jakie Jog T-shirts that had been designed at Banana Graphics. The cartoon characterization of

Jacob wearing his signature green frog rain boots made me cry. He had a reputation for wearing them all the time, even in the middle of summer. On the back of the shirts, it said, "If you think running is hard, you should try chemo."

Kids slipped down inflated water slides and tossed beanbags at the dunk tank dropping Dave at least a dozen times. Jojo and Jess enjoyed that booth the most. But not Jacob. He became too exhausted, and I took him to the air conditioned media box where a place had been prepared for him and then I returned to the track.

"Mommy, where's my chips?"

His voice boomed over the loud speaker, and I could see Jacob in the window, laughing. In his decadron induced hunger, all he wanted to do was eat. Thanks to Route 66 restaurant, which had been one of Justin's favorite eateries, there were plenty of hamburgers and hot dogs to choose from. Anyone hearing Jacob call their name was beckoned to the air-conditioned press booth, where he sat like a prince on his throne, calling to his servants below. It was obvious that he was enjoying this momentary state of power. This was the perfect way for him to participate in the day's festivities without overstressing him.

"Will Mrs. Patterson please come up here?"

He sounded like an announcer at a carnival. Cathy Patterson ran by me on her way to the media box.

"I guess I am the chosen one." She smiled.

Booths were set up to sell everything from green rubber Jakie Jog bracelets and snow cones to hot dogs and T-shirts. The view from above was impressive.

There were at least a thousand people there. I watched Jacob to make sure he was tolerating the experience well. After all, he had already spent more time in a hospital than I cared to think about, and I didn't want to add to that list of visits. He was getting tired, and Auntie Cathie offered to take him home with her kids so he could cool off and play with his cousins. He was happier than he had been in days.

The event was the single most overwhelming gift of charity I had ever received, both in love and currency. All of our needs were met; Jacob's supplements, medical co-payments, parking fees, eating out, and lost wages were no longer a worry. At the end of the day, when the totals were in, Kathy Gold stood next to me as my knees buckled and I had to sit down. I couldn't take it all in; so much love and generosity in the midst of so much fear and pain.

As the event winded down, I walked around, thanking everyone I could find. I bowed and shook hands. I'd have kissed feet too if it helped convey the gratitude I felt. If love could be measured monetarily, then we were truly loved. It was a huge relief to feel the embrace of so many kind-hearted people through financial support, well wishes, and prayers.

Jacob spent the next two weeks in the arms of his cousins. Mikala, who is four years older than him, held him in her arms like a monkey mother, comforting him, preening his hair, jumping to his every need. Emily, two years younger than her sister, brought him cool drinks and fresh Play-Doh, always ready to help. Isaiah, the youngest of them all, danced around, ever entertaining.

As treatments continued, I came to the conclusion that one mercy seat carving was absolutely wrong: "Money is useful but not worth anything in the face of death." Money was exactly what you need in this modern world when facing death, especially when it comes to a child, both to try and keep the kid alive as that chapter plays out and also to bury them if that is how the story ends. Today, cancer battles are a lesson in financial crises, as one parent quits work to take care of the sick child while, at the same time, expenses increase. Money is the weapon of choice when you need to kick death in the teeth and slow him down for a while.

The community's generosity continued when an employee of United Oil, a private petroleum vendor, saw our story on the local news one evening. Two boys with leukemia seemed unjust to him, and he called me, offering free gasoline to help us with our trips to the hospital while Jacob was on treatment. This kind of generosity from complete strangers humbled me. I was thankful to tears as the weight of how to manage life continued to lift.

Grocery gift cards from the Michael Hoefflin Foundation (MHF) and people everywhere come in the mail. Cash, checks, movie tickets, and all kinds of thoughtful gestures were poured out on us. This was exactly what we needed. This is exactly what most families in our position need: practical, cold, hard cash and lots of love and prayers and people to help manage it all. When a child is diagnosed with cancer, life is changed forever. It is not fixed in a day like a laceration, sewn up; or a week, like a cold, "Take this and call me in the morning"; or even a month or two, like a fracture, "Come back in six weeks and we will remove the cast." With cancer, it takes months and years and, for us, decades.

Dave and I were speechless and exhausted most of the time. The drive back and forth to CHLA almost every day became routine, as did watching blood drip through IV tubing into Jacob's port and holding him as he cried while receiving intramuscular injections in both thighs. We used numbing cream called LMX on the injection sight to ease the pain. This topical anesthetic, which I applied to areas of Jacob's skin where he would be poked—like his portacath, his lower back, and his thighs—ran out much faster than one might imagine. It must be applied at least thirty minutes prior to an injection, but if the procedure was delayed, it had to be reapplied. It did seem to help numb the pain, so we used it. It was $70 for a tube the size of a sample of toothpaste and was not covered by our insurance. It occured to me as I reached into my wallet to pay for it at the pharmacy that I was not actually the one paying for this pain-relieving wonder; our community was. Being able to relieve Jacob's pain relieved my pain. People who had made it possible for me to buy this anesthetic were like my own LMX cream.

Blood Brothers

Treatments continued, and we took it all in as it unfolded. Jessica and Jojo tried to stay connected to what they were doing before the earth fell away from their feet. They ran cross-country and went to school. They tired of being the sisters of a brother with cancer. They appreciated it when people asked how they were doing, but it was all too much sometimes. Life was not normal for them, but they put on brave faces and tried not to think about death too much. Jojo came to the clinic with us from time to time. She and Jacob were inseparable before leukemia. Jojo was an eighth grader in junior high when all of this started and I could see that she hurt for him. She took on the role of caregiver, and exhibited many of the same qualities that Justin had displayed to her when she was little: changing clothes, helping baths, playing games.

For Jessica, who was a senior at Canyon, it was tough to see it all again. She was eleven years old when Justin died and was reliving a vivid nightmare, one she remembered too well. She had been voted Homecoming Queen the year Jacob was diagnosed, her senior year. Even so, she became weary of being the sister who had a brother with cancer again.

"I am so tired of telling people how Jacob is feeling. It is nice of them to ask, but I just can't talk about it anymore," she had said one day after school.

We were all standing in our own place of reverence and fear, in our own place of worship, trying to figure out who we were to a God who would allow this much suffering. Each of us was leaning with our haunches on a shelf while life's proceedings unfolded before us. We knew the routine. It was like a long Sunday Mass with genuflecting, earnest prayers, aching knees, and an unpalatable Eucharist. We were in the middle of it, hoping to endure each day without buckling under the weight of life while the fear of death sat heavy on our laps.

Lisa Solis DeLong

By November, we were as accustomed to living with cancer as we could be. Jacob could not stop eating. The Decadron did this, caused intense food cravings. The first time Justin had experienced these cravings, he woke me up at three in the morning, asking for a grilled cheese sandwich. These late-night satiations were mild compared to Jacob's daily routine. It was not unusual for him to wolf down a barbeque dinner, lick the mashed potatoes from his fingers, eye the next serving, throw up, wipe his mouth, and ask for more. It was a sickening cycle of consumption and excretion.

These kinds of cravings were notorious among other families with childhood cancer experiences. In group when we compared notes: little Abbey demanded a specific kind of fried chicken to which her father would get in the car and get it or face her wrath; or five-year-old Manny's craving for Doritos, or the most common "I want pizza" or "chips"; these comparisons were the one thing we could laugh about. Managing healthy dietary choices under these circumstances had not gotten any easier since I first dealt with them with Justin. Kids get extremely picky about the thing they crave and demand it. I heard an adult under steroid therapy appropriately call it "Roid Rage." At least Jacob's cravings were not waking us up in the middle of the night.

Dave and the girls remained focused on school and sports, while Jacob and I prepared for the holidays. He was obsessed with Playmobile toys and enjoyed going online, searching their website and picking out what he wanted for Christmas. He had been eagerly awaiting the release of a new dragon castle set which I'd promised he could order. Receiving a new toy in the mail gave him something to look forward to, which was evidenced by his running to the front window every time he heard the "brown truck" come up the street. The problem was, he had just received the hardest round of treatment—delayed intensification—and it could kill him.

We were warned that this regimen would wipe out his immune system. It had when Justin went through it the first time, but he recovered. He didn't make it that far the second time. Keeping Jacob away from crowds was a must.

He seemed to be tolerating the treatment well. He wasn't throwing up as much and he had a decent level of energy. One evening he and Jojo sat on the couch, playing video games, when Dave and I decided to go out to dinner alone. We weren't ten minutes into our date when my phone rang. Jojo's voice was tense. "He feels warm, Mom, and he has a bloody nose." I put down my margarita, apologized to the waiter, and we sped home. Spiking a fever was an instant ticket to the ER. He'd had bloody noses off and on since diagnosis, a side effect Justin never experienced. When we got home, Jojo was holding a tissue to his nose, applying pressure. "This one just won't stop," she said as I took over. It makes me tear up every time I see this scene in my memory—Jojo the veteran caregiver at fourteen!

This was how chemo was—it killed cells at will, leaving us guessing, always putting out unseen fires. Even though Jacob received a unit of blood the day before and his cheeks were rosy, there was no way of knowing how fast his counts were falling.

Blood Brothers

It was the eve of Thanksgiving Day, our sixth trip to the ER. We knew the routine. Dave picked up Jacob and put him in his jog stroller; I placed a mask on Jacob, and he pulled his leopard print blanket over the canopy of the stroller to hide. Jojo handed Jacob the basin, and he held it under the blanket. My anxiety level rose as serous blood oozed soaking tissue after pink-stained tissue. We checked in at the front desk and made our way through the CHLA corridors to the waiting room of the ER where at least thirty children were waiting to be seen. I felt irritated until I remembered the South American woman I'd met in support group last month. She was a tiny woman; at five feet tall, I towered over her. Through an interpreter she had shared how she walked; hitch hiked and bartered her way to the United States in order to find treatment for her five-year-old daughter, who had a brain tumor. "There was no hope for her if I stayed in my country, so I started walking."

She conveyed how terrifying the ordeal had been as she crossed a river, which nearly swept her and her daughter away. "I thought we were going to drown when a man pulled me out of the water. There were bodies floating by. I had to cover my daughter's eyes." I couldn't imagine what half of these people had been through to get here.

What I did know was that the waiting room was like a minefield to Jacob. Even one germ could kill him, so Dave waited with him down the hall as I walked past the crowd. "My son is on treatment for leukemia," I told the security guard, who waved me to the front of the line. Playing the leukemia card came in handy at the CHLA ER.

Jacob, still hiding under his blanket, found that his mask and bloody nose were impossible opponents. He lifted the mask to wad new cones of twisted tissue into his nostrils. He did this so often that wearing the mask was not feasible, leaving him vulnerable to airborne disease. Dave and Jojo waited for my signal to bring him to the triage door.

I was called to the window to check in. An attractive brunette tapped at the keyboard with three-quarter-inch fingernails, which looked like mini Picasso's. Each one was a blend of blues and magentas with swirls of white, which must have been created by an artist using an air brush and fine instruments. I found myself staring, watching them tap dance on the keys like a stage scene from CATS as her fingers glided and hopped in glittered finery.

"I'm sorry for staring, but your nails are amazing."

"Thanks." The tapping stopped.

"May I see them for a second?" I asked.

"Sure."

They were even more amazing up close. On her nails, there were sunrises and sunsets, moons and stars—the universe at her finger tips.

She returned them to the keyboard, "Date of birth?"

I was quickened to respond.

"Any allergies?"

"No," I said, feeling guilty for having taken a moment of indulgence.

I wished I had the universe at my fingertips. If I had, I'd get the hell out of there. Perhaps that was why the woman behind the desk wore them. She sat in a room full of sick children, night after long night, her artful nails typing in the name of one sick child after another, all the while breathing in the airborne diseases they may have carried with them. The air all around her was an invisible septic tank.

Quick work in the ER by the skilled nurses and docs got Jacob's port accessed and lab results fast. The ones who worked there—spending twelve-hour-plus shifts in a space too small for the numbers of kids they saw, bumping elbows as they jockeyed for space in the crowded work station—were my saviors.

He was admitted to Four East again, and his white cell count, also known as the absolute neutrophil count or ANC, was dangerously low. He received antibiotics immediately and was monitored for sepsis. His platelets were low so he was given more. He had no appetite and began having black, liquid stools. The next day, his belly began to swell (ascites) and his arms and feet looked puffy (edema). He was not on Decadron at the time, so this was unusual. His urine output started to decrease, even though he was receiving continuous IV fluids. One day of watching this progression and the nurse in me started seeing it: a fluid shift. I told the medical team that I was concerned, and it was like being in one of those dreams when you are drowning in a pool and people are walking around, and you are calling out for help. They all smile as if to say you'll be fine, but you keep sinking and the water keeps rising, and soon you are gasping for air.

Time moves slowly in the hospital. Jacob and I sat in bed and watched the USC/Notre Dame football game. Dave had gotten tickets and took the girls in an attempt to spend much needed time with them. He had his phone and was closer to us than if he had stayed home. Jacob got a kick out of looking for Dave and the girls in the crowd. He was a budding Trojan fan, so the game made a nice distraction.

Jacob's urine output decreased to less than 30 cc/hour, which was serious, and I asked if he would begin receiving a diuretic. I wanted to know what was going on, but I was told that his blood work showed he was dehydrated so they could not use diuretics.

As I had feared in the beginning, Dr. Siegel was out of town, and I began losing faith in the team who was handling things.

I called Dr. Siegel's assistant and told her, "If I don't see the whites of his eyes today, I am gonna freak."

He called me from a taxi in Chicago within the hour. I told him what I saw, and he assured me he was on it. An hour later, they had a diagnosis: veno-occlusive disease (VOD). I had never heard of it. I didn't know if anyone else on his team had thought of this diagnosis, but Jacob's symptoms were finally given a name, and that made me feel better. VOD was "very unusual," they said, which I was so tired of hearing when it came to my boys that I wanted to slap the person who said it. Everything about leukemia was unusual. For someone who had received the kinds of chemo that Jacob had, VOD was almost unheard of.

One of his doctors told me, "It is more common in kids who are going through bone marrow transplants because they receive such high doses of chemo. We weren't looking for this problem in Jacob." I immediately thought of Justin, since the cause of his death was never pinned down. No bacteria or virus ever grew from the blood cultures they had done. No one ever had an explanation for the cause of the ARDS, which caused his lungs to fill with fluid.

Dr. Siegel returned the next day and explained that Jacob's liver had become so toxic that the portal vein, which was located in the liver, was shunting fluid backward. The liver, in its rebellion, was also holding onto platelets. No matter how fast they infused them into Jacob's IV, his platelet count continued to fall. Platelets are what stop people from bleeding to death. Jacob's body was spiraling out of control, and he was at risk of multiple organ failures and bleeding out. He received over twenty units of various blood products in forty-eight hours. His gums wouldn't stop bleeding.

"Mommy, I keep tasting blood," he said as I held the emesis basin up to his mouth. "Spit it out, Jacob," I said. He did, and I was frightened at the sight of the bright red color and the quantity, more than I had ever seen with typical brushing of teeth.

I understood part of what was happening but lived in real time I didn't know that his risk of mortality was rising by the minute. The nurse packed his gums with gauze soaked in prostaglandins to slow the bleeding. Jacob started having difficulty breathing, and they began giving him oxygen through a mask, which was annoying to him but brought his oxygen saturation levels from the mid eighties up to the low nineties. Chest x-rays confirmed that his lungs were being squeezed by fluid filling the pleural cavity. It was not actually in his lungs, like it had been with Justin, but the competition for space was making it difficult for his lungs to stay inflated, and his breathing was severely compromised.

Jacob's body became so swollen that he looked like the Pillsbury Doughboy: bald, white, and round. I touched his shin, and my finger left a dent—pitting edema. This condition caused him wincing pain when he was touched. Dave and I hung on every word he spoke as his voice became a whisper. We guarded him like wolves, growling if anyone touched him too hard. This was where my respect for nurses, which was already off the charts, increased dramatically. Our oncology nurses became critical care nurses and had to provide serious, complex, treatments that required very close monitoring and the use of extensive medication protocols and therapies. Jacob's room was turned into a mini-ICU with heart monitors, multiple IV pumps, and a pressurized oxygen system. I wondered if they had any idea that they would be pushed to their limits that day. Jacob's nurses ran to hang bag after bag of blood, platelets, plasma and antibiotics. He received over twenty doses of blood products. They checked his vital signs and lab results. Keeping Jacob alive at this point required a group effort. A doctor from ICU came to see him. They had no beds available in the ICU, or Jacob would have been put in one by then.

"I'm watching him closely," he said. "He is working very hard to breathe, so he might need to be intubated."

Not this again. This cannot be happening, I thought, and just like it did with Justin, the idea of Jacob being intubated raised my fear level to a point of inconceivability. I couldn't take it in. The word *intubate* floated around my mind and entered in slow and unclear syllables until Dave and I were escorted into a conference room where Dr. Siegel spoke in slow, steady tones.

"Jacob is very sick," he said. "You need to prepare yourselves."

I did not yet know that the morbidity rate for children with this disease was ninety percent. I only knew that Jacob was fighting for his life and it didn't seem fair.

Dave held my hand and I his. I asked question after question about VOD and why nobody had been looking for it and how it could be stopped.

"If his liver doesn't start releasing platelets in the next twelve hours, he might not make it," he said. "It is possible that his body will turn this around. But given that he is not holding on to platelets, we cannot be certain he will survive this."

How many times had Dr. Siegel had to say these words to a mother like me? How many parents have sat in this bleak, white room hearing those most dreaded words even once? I could not help but second-guess God's mercy here.

"We are doing everything we can," Dr. Siegel assured us. "We will be watching his platelet count closely, and he *has* to start urinating. Keep your fingers crossed."

Fingers? That's it?

We left the conference room weak from terror. Dave said, "Fingers crossed? That's it?" He did what he always did when he had been broken and laid out and helpless: he called everyone he could to pray. E-mails were sent, and cell phones rang.

"Pray for our Jacob. He needs a miracle."

Once again, the voices of the faithful, and the unfaithful flowed outward. "I'm not the praying type but I was on my knees for Jacob," we were told more than once.

Dave made phone calls and I walked down the hall, away from Four East. At the end, there was a floor-to-ceiling window. I had stared out this window many times. From there I could see the infamous white Hollywood sign, the dome of the Griffith Park Observatory, and the CHLA research buildings across the street, which housed Justin's cells. This was where God and I had it out, like I did when I'd received the news of Justin's diagnosis, or his relapses. When it was Justin lying in the hospital bed, dying, I knew the odds and I was able to release him. This time I was more desperate. Jacob's leukemia was not high risk, his cells were round, and he was not even finished with treatment yet. I begged for Jacob's life to be spared, to take me instead, to take anything. I screamed at the creator of heaven and earth for doing this to one of my sons again.

"How could you?" I said in desperate whispered prayers. "Why can't you just leave my boy alone?" like he was some kind of bully and Jacob needed me to step in.

I was crying, my head hanging between my arms, my hands pressed against the clear, glass windowpane. After several minutes, my ranting ended, and I felt like I had nothing left.

As I stood there at the end of that long corridor, I began to feel a strange sense of euphoria. This surprised me. It felt good. I could feel myself communicating; but I had no words. I was silent, my eyes were closed, and I had stopped crying. What I heard deep inside astonished me.

Jacob is going to live.

If peace came in liquid form, I would have been soaked. I didn't know how I knew Jacob would live, but I believed it to my core, and I felt myself smile. I sat with it a few minutes and let it settle. I wanted to run in to his room and shout, "He's going to live! He's gonna make it!" But I knew I would sound crazy. The assurance was so powerful that I thanked God and Jesus and Justin as though Jacob was already healed. I walked slow and steady, one step at a time, back to Jacob's room.

He was struggling for breath. His oxygen saturation levels were dipping into the mid eighties, which was not good. They should have been in the nineties. A portable chest X-ray was done, which showed so much fluid around Jacob's lungs that a chest tube was suggested to drain the fluid but not chosen because his platelets were so low it would have caused uncontrollable bleeding. I could have panicked then, but I knew what I knew, and what I didn't. I touched Jacob, and his skin was still taut. He was in pain. Even so, I felt the need to close my eyes and whisper, "Thank you for healing him."

The ICU doc came by again, reassessing him. The nurses worked nonstop. They were skillful, capable, and attentive. Their level of expertise was much higher than mine, and through that terrible night I appreciated every masterful IV change, every bag of plate-lets, and blood, and plasma. I saw the way they checked Jacob's ID band and touched him tenderly. I heard the way they opened the door to his room with as little disruption as possible, ever vigilant that any stimulation was adding to my over stimulated child's stress level lying in the bed. I watched them, and I was ready to pounce if they made a mistake. I was one of them, and I knew enough to rip into them if they blew it; but they never did. Jacob was so sick that I felt scared for them—the ones who were keeping him alive. I knew that Jacob's medical team was made up of human beings, vulnerable, fragile, susceptible people just like me. I was rooting for them. I knew what it was like to have to stick a needle into another person's flesh and cause them pain. I was familiar with what it was like to be the nurse who gives the wrong medication and has to face the error. I knew how bad it felt to fail at keeping a child alive.

Dave and I sat and waited and watched Jacob's every breath. Our prayers were constant. I held on to the powerful feeling of peace I'd felt in the corridor. Doing so eased my stress level in between bouts of reality based doubt. There was no reading of books or light conversations. The only thing that mattered was Jacob's life.

At around midnight, Jacob said, "Can you take that thing off? It's bugging me." And then he pulled off his oxygen mask and said in a clear voice, "I have to go pee-pee."

Yellow gold! We practically knocked each other over trying to get to him first. There was nothing on earth more valuable to us than that warm liquid waste. The tinkle of urine filling the plastic urinal was the most soothing sound we'd heard in days. Dave and I danced around the room in a tight hug.

The pulse oximeter probe had been strapped to Jacob's toe for days, and he began to feel well enough to complain about it. Little by little, Jacob's oxygen levels began to improve. Slowly, they started to hit 90 percent and then 95 percent.

He peed, and then in a few minutes he peed again and then again. Jacob was sitting up, smiling, peeing so often that we had to have two urinals. Dave helped him fill it and then handed it to me to empty. We were a pee-pee relay team, and Jacob laughed at our routine.

His gums stopped bleeding, and morning lab results revealed that his platelet counts were starting to rise. His liver was letting go. It was recovering. Every bit of good news, offered confirmation that what I'd heard was true.

That morning, Jacob made a request, "Can you bring the drawing of JD? The one that Auntie Lori sketched for me. I want to hang it, right there." He pointed to an area on the wall directly in front of his bed.

"Sure, Jakie Boy, anything you want. What made you think about JD's picture right now?" I asked.

"I don't know. I just want it," he said in a matter-of-fact tone.

A repeat chest X-ray revealed that most of the fluid was gone. In one day he went from near death to near normal, and the doctors couldn't believe it. They checked and rechecked the identification numbers and name because it looked as though the X-ray belonged to someone else. But it was Jacob's. I heard myself sigh over and over again as if my breaths were releasing, "Thank you. Thank you," with every exhale.

A friend stopped by that afternoon. He had not been able to sleep that night.

"I tossed and turned and thought about Jacob all night. The Lord was telling me that he was very sick, very near death. And he kept showing me a filter, like a car filter, a pump. He showed me that the filter needed fixing. I prayed for Jacob all night long. What happened?"

Jacob was sitting up, playing with Play-Doh.

I told my friend what had happened and how I just knew Jacob would be okay and how strange and crazy the whole experience had been. He listened to me spill about the deep spiritual things that had been going on and how this knowing that I had received with Jacob had come true. "I had them with Justin too," I told him. "I had it when Justin was born on the day I held him in my arms and felt his breath for the first time, and I knew that something tragic would happen to him. I knew that the heavier rounds of chemo would kill

Justin, and it did. I saw Justin's death in a dream before it occurred; and then, with Jacob, I knew he would live."

My friend assured me that I was not alone in these spirit-filled experiences.

"I've had them since I was very young. Many people do," he said.

It felt comforting to converse with someone so open minded and kind. He was older and wiser, and I valued his presence in my life at this critical juncture.

Jacob's recovery was so fast that the doctors and nurses were commenting on how amazed they were.

One resident said, "I saw yesterday's chest X-ray, and I thought it belonged to a different patient."

Another came in and said, "Wow! Jacob, you look so good. All that fluid is gone."

"Can you believe it?" I said.

"That's the power of Lasix for you," she replied.

"And divine power," I said. "If you ask me, this was a miracle."

I knew what I had seen and the conversations I'd had. I heard the whisperings in the sanctuary I called Childrens Hospital Los Angeles, where people with skillful yet limited abilities worked hard using medicine to save lives. But they were not omnipotent. If they were, all children would live. Their ability to affect outcomes like Jacob's was beyond the realm of human understanding. I did get JD's picture as Jacob had asked.

I hung it on the wall at eye level as Jacob directed, "A little higher, Mom. Okay, right there."

I crawled in bed with him and warmed my feet with his. As we stared at Justin's face, I contemplated the mystery behind one son's death and the other's survival, content to sit awhile with both.

It was Christmas 2006. Jacob's blood counts were normalizing to the point of being safe to be in public places on a limited basis. On

Blood Brothers

Christmas Eve, we went to church together for the first time in six months. The sound of the choir singing Christmas carols touched me. This in contrast to the sights and sounds of hospital life, where it was quite possible that a much-loved child was dying, made me weep. I appreciated the ability to attend worship services and celebrate the life of Christ. White lights sparkled, a Christmas tree stood poised, and poinsettias colored the scene red. To waste time fearful over Jacob's future that day was unacceptable. Dave was at my left, standing and singing in his off-key voice. He was belting out "Oh Holy Night," so loudly it was almost embarrassing. "The stars are brightly shining…" Jacob was at my right, Joelle was next to him, and Jessica was next to her. "It is the night of the dear Saviors birth…" We glanced at each other. "A thrill of hope, the weary world rejoices." We got this, each in our own way. I looked back at Dave, and tears were streaming down his face. "For yonder breaks a new and glorious morn."

On our way out of church, we sang "Oh night divine, oh night divine."

Our family was like a chain that would not be broken. We got into the car and began our way home when whispering erupted in the backseat.

"Mom, it's Christmas Eve," Jessica said. "Can we get a puppy?"

"Yeah, Mom. Can we?" Jojo pleaded in the same voice she used to beg for ice cream or cookies.

"Please, Mom? Please, Papa?" from Jacob. "All we want for Christmas is a puppy. Please?"

"A puppy would be a great way to celebrate," I said because I loved animals and the thought of silken fur and puppy breath lit me up.

On and on we went until Dave conceded.

"Okay, okay. Jacob still has three years of treatment to go, and he could use a buddy. You can get a puppy, but drop me off at home first." Dave's response was as close to enthusiastic as he could conjure up over having another mouth to feed.

"Yeah! Let's go," the kids said almost in unison.

We dropped off Dave, stepped inside the pet store, and spent two hours playing with puppies while Christmas music filled the air.

"I want this one." Jessica held a wiggling teacup Yorkie to her face as it licked her chin with a passion known only to puppies.

"No. Not that one," Jojo said. "This one, the miniature pincer. Look how cute she is."

She was jumping all over the visiting room like a super ball.

"I like this one," Jacob said. "The papillon. Look at his big ears. And look. He likes me." The puppy was gently licking his chin.

"Papillon means butterfly in French," I said, recalling what a friend of mine told me about hers.

Curled up on Jacob's lap, looking up at him, was a little white fluff with jackrabbit ears. He looked like a cotton ball with wings.

Managing sibling matters suddenly became a delicate operation: please the girls or please Jacob. I had envisioned all three kids falling in love with one pup, not three; but I should have known it would come to this.

Which puppy to choose, to take home and love, to have a future with, to be our celebratory canine? The kids whined and pleaded their cases; but I couldn't think, so I made them wait out front. When I thought of everything I had witnessed that year, this decision wasn't that tough. I was the one who had been in the hospital for days and weeks and crying at the foot of Jacob's bed. I was going to pick the dog I wanted. I would be the one feeding him and picking up his poop. If I hadn't learned that by now, there was something wrong with me. The teacup was too delicate and high maintenance. The Min-Pin was too hyper.

"Oh, sure. Pick the one that Jacob wants," the girls complained, and Jacob smiled as they saw me exit the store holding the cotton ball with wings.

There was bickering, and I was at once annoyed and content because this felt normal.

Blood Brothers

The girls whined, but Jessica got to hold the Papillon puppy first, and each one took their turn in order. He licked their faces and nibbled their fingers, and there was a chorus of laughter in the backseat. There was peace among the ranks and by the time we got home we were in love.

Lisa Solis DeLong

Meeting Pete

"Mom, I think I'm gonna throw up!"

These were not the words I wanted to hear while driving on the frenzied Hollywood Freeway on our way to the California Science Center. It was Jacob's first "field trip" since leukemia treatments began eight months earlier when I began homeschooling him. His immune system counts were safe again after a rollercoaster of ups and downs the previous month.

The girls had preferred school over a trip to a "boring" museum. Dave groaned at the idea and gladly went to work. It had been weeks since the chemo had made Jacob sick. Mona, our family friend who had adopted Jacob as her own, was sitting in the backseat at Jacob's request. She now frantically grabbed for a plastic bag, but vomit waits for no one. Jacob threw up all over his jeans and T-shirt.

While Jacob retched and coughed, I took the Vermont exit, cut through traffic, and pulled over to the side of the road.

"Are you okay, big guy?" I asked.

Tears filled his green eyes. "Mom," he asked, "can we still go to the museum?" He wanted to see the insect exhibit and the nature movie at the IMAX.

At this point in treatment, it didn't make sense for Jacob to get sick. He wasn't on hard chemo anymore, and I couldn't understand why this would have happened. Could this be the beginning of a bigger problem, something I couldn't identify yet, as had happened so many times before? I reached back to feel Jacob's forehead as Mona wiped him down. No fever. I acted calm, but inside I was flaming mad.

Lord! You've already taken Justin. Can't Jacob catch a break? Is it too much to ask to go easy on us this time? Just one day without a glitch? Isn't Jacob having leukemia too enough? I just don't understand you! Why does life have to be so hard?

I was glad I'd invited Mona, a veteran ICU nurse. She first saw Jacob at one of Jessica's track meets when Jacob was only three years old. He played around on the field while his big sister ran her heart out on the track. Mona called me repeatedly after Jacob was diagnosed. It felt good to have someone to talk to, who knew as much, if not more, about leukemia than I did.

"Please let me sit with him," Mona would say. "I want to help."

They fell in love the first time Mona came to see him in the hospital.

"You and Dave go get dinner," she said. "You need a break."

She was right. When we returned from dinner that night, we found them sitting together, Jacob practically purring in Mona's arms using her large, soft bosoms as his pillow. Mona oozes kindness, even in the middle of a mess on the side of the road.

I, on the other hand, was still frantically trying to come up with a new plan. In the midst of my roadside mental tirade, a thought occurred to me that might actually work. The University of Southern California, only a few miles away, was across the street from the

Science Center. I remembered visiting Dave back when he was a Trojan in the eighties, when I lived in the nursing dorms at LA County just a few miles away. He always needed something from the bookstore in those days. Surely they would have sweat pants and a T-shirt to fit Jacob; and if he felt okay, we could still make it to the museum. Jacob smiled when I proposed the plan.

"Yeah," he said. "I don't have any USC shirts. Can we go? Can we?"

He and Dave had watched plenty of Trojan football games while in the hospital that fall. They lay in the hospital bed, Dave cheering, Jacob mesmerized by their mascot, Traveler, the noble white steed, complete with regal Trojan warrior astride, who appeared whenever a touchdown was scored.

I looked at Mona for support. She gave her approval and wrapped her arms around Jacob, and I headed for Exposition Parkway. I saw the cluster of museums on one side, the university on the other. I was driving and praying, *Please don't let Jakie down. Please don't let him throw up anymore. I don't know how much more disappointment he can take.*

As soon as Mona and I got out of the car, we went into action, peeling off the soiled clothes, cleaning Jacob with baby wipes, both of us nurses immune to the stench of vomit. Jacob—standing on the sidewalk, stripped down to his SpongeBob underpants and white socks, cars whizzing by—grinned shyly.

"Look, Jakie. I'm Stellaluna's mom," I said, picturing myself as a mother bat from one of Jacob's favorite books in which a baby fruit bat gets separated from her mother.

Wrapping my blanket wings around him tight, Jacob leaned in to me, smelling sweet and sour, like he did as an infant after a diaper change. I picked him up, blanket and all, and placed him in the stroller. With legs too weak from chemo, he liked the cocoon of his three-wheel jog stroller, especially now, as he wore nothing but his underwear beneath the blanket. We crossed the street and made our way toward USC.

The campus welcomed us with its gargoyle-topped buildings next to sleek modern ones. Aged shade trees stood still as coeds on bicycles cruised by. I used to love coming here to visit Dave, that easy life before marriage and children, when our biggest worries were whether to take bio or poli sci seemed distant, not my own. Disoriented, I wasn't sure where the bookstore was. I asked a passerby.

"Hang a left at Tommy Trojan," she said, wearing a denim mini skirt and tight, pink T-shirt.

We entered the bookstore and found a pair of cardinal sweatpants with USC in gold and white printed down the left leg and a long-sleeved T-shirt to match.

"This is the best day of my life!" Jacob proclaimed as I set the new clothes on his lap. He fingered the gold print as if it were precious metal.

I decided to call Dave, the man with the Trojan fight song ringtone. We had been through so much together that I knew he'd want to know what was going on. I detected a hint of jealousy in his voice when I told him we were shopping at the bookstore.

We entered the bathroom. All three stalls were empty. While we washed Jacob down in the corner, a woman entered. Her dark hair fell at her shoulders. A vinyl badge dangled around her neck. She smiled when she saw Jacob standing there in his underwear, his portacath intravenous line, a pink-stained, two-inch scar under the skin beneath his left clavicle; puffy belly; and pale skin—telltale signs of illness.

"Hi. I'm Angelica," she said. "Do you need any help?" We told her what had happened on the way there and how Jacob was being treated for leukemia.

"Do you like your new clothes, Jacob?" she asked.

He lowered his eyes and grinned shyly and nodded.

"How old are you?"

"Seven," he said.

"My little girl is seven too. She loves football. How about you? Do you like football?"

"Yes," Jacob tipped his head shyly.

We chatted for a while, and then she turned toward the door. "Can you hang on a minute?" she asked, reaching for the handle.

I nodded.

"I'm about to make his day," she said as she swung the door open.

Mona and I looked at each other, shrugged our shoulders, and helped Jacob slip on his new pants.

A few minutes later, Angelica reentered the bathroom. Jacob, wearing his new gear, smiled as she placed an authentic leather USC football in his hands.

"This is signed by thirty of the football players and will be worth quite a lot of money someday," she said. "I'd like you to have it."

Jacob smiled in silence, staring at the ball. One minute we were sopping up vomit, and now we were standing in the heart of USC with new clothes, a football, and a woman accurately named.

"Wow!" Mona said. "That was so nice!"

I touched the white threads of the ball. "Thank you," I said. "How did you do that?"

"I know all the players," Angelica said. "I'm in charge of getting them their books." Reaching for the door, she said, "I have another idea. Hold on. I'll be right back."

As Angelica left the bathroom, I called Dave and told him about the autographed football.

"What?" he said, "Are you kidding me? That's great! Does Jakie like it?"

"He said he'd let you touch it if you are nice to him," I joked.

"Do you know who signed it?"

"No, but now do you wish you had come to the museum with us?" I teased.

Angelica came back beaming, and I hung up the phone.

"Jacob," she said, "How would you like to meet some of the guys on the team?"

Mona and I glanced at each other. "Now?" I asked.

"Follow me and we'll get you checked out of here and head for Heritage Hall."

We followed her out of the bookstore. Feeling a bit starstruck at the thought of meeting the players, I couldn't help but wonder why they would be willing to meet us. We were simple strangers coming off of the street. These were some of the nation's best college athletes.

We made our way to Heritage Hall and entered through the Walk of Fame Hallway, a sacred tunnel lined with life-sized photos of famous football players: Reggie Bush, Marcus Allen, Matt Leinhart. You could practically see the testosterone lifting from the print. Feeling like I was shrinking, I continued pushing Jacob as we entered the athlete-only zone, where guys with thighs as big as boulders squatted down and shook hands with Jacob.

"Hey, bud. What's up?"

Burly, strapping, handsome, and young, I thought. *Man, this beats the heck out of a museum.*

Maybe I was getting a little carried away, but I turned to one of the players standing next to me and said, "Do you mind if I feel your bicep?"

It was like holding a warm Frisbee-sized river rock with a pulse. At five feet tall, I was dumbstruck by the size of these guys. Jacob giggled as he sat in the safety of his stroller. I couldn't get over how nice everyone was.

As we made our rounds, gathering more autographs for Jacob's football, a man in dark slacks and collared shirt approached us. Smiling, he put his hand out.

"Hi. I'm Jason, the assistant athletic director. I heard you had a pretty rough day." Then he squatted down to stroller level. "Hi, Jacob," he said. "Are you feeling a little better now?"

Jacob nodded. He asked about Jacob's diagnosis as a few of the guys hung around.

"Hey," he said, "I have an idea. How'd you like to meet Coach Carroll?"

Mona and I nodded exaggerated nods at Jacob to make sure he gave the right answer. The next thing I knew, we were being escorted upstairs to football headquarters. The guy with the biceps picked up Jacob, stroller and all, and carried him up the stairs.

I called Dave again from the stairway. "You're not gonna believe this. We're on our way to meet Pete Carroll!"

A pause and then, "Are you kidding me? What the heck is going on down there?"

I gave him a quick update. "*Now* do you wish you'd come to the museum with us?"

We walked past Heisman trophies on white pedestals in the lobby and entered into a large room that looked more like a comfortable den than an office: rich leather sofas; a large, flat-screen TV mounted on the wall; trophies; framed football jerseys; and a wall-sized mural of the Rose Bowl. Jacob climbed out of the stroller and onto one of the sofas. Assistant coaches stopped and shook hands with Jacob. Someone handed him a T-shirt.

Another said, "Get Jacob a hat," as secretaries offered popcorn and water.

One of the players stopped by and sat on the sofa, close to Jacob.

"What do you do?" Jacob asked.

"I'm a running back," he said, putting out his hand to give him a low five.

Jacob placed his hand on top, and they stayed that way for a moment. The player's hand, large, dark, calloused, and powerful, was enormous compared to Jacob's, which was small, pale, and soft.

"What does that mean?" Jacob said.

"It means I run around a lot and try to catch the ball without getting smashed," he said and smiled.

After visiting for a few minutes, Jacob needed to lie down. "I'm starting to not feel so good, Mom."

I looked around the room for a trashcan.

"I'm hungry," he said, allaying my fears. Spying a gumball machine on the desk in front of him, he said, "Can I have one of those?"

Three people came back with handfuls of gumballs.

And then in walked Pete Carroll, casual and welcoming, in worn blue jeans and a gray sweatshirt, his wavy hair tousled and gray. He immediately sat on the leather sofa, as close to Jacob as he could. Putting his arm around my frail boy, he looked Jacob in the eyes.

"How you doin,' buddy?" he asked. "I heard you weren't feeling very well earlier today."

Jacob nodded and leaned in to him like a puppy hoping to get stroked. They sat in that warm embrace for several minutes as though this man, who ran the most successful college football program in the nation, had all the time in the world.

Good Lord, I thought. *Has the universe flipped?* There were so few times when I felt sure of what was going on, but in that moment, I was certain: Jacob was in good hands.

"Hey, Jacob," Pete said, "let's go into my office. I wanna show you something."

Pete helped Jacob off the sofa and held his hand as we left the waiting area and went into his office.

He showed Jacob around the room: books on oak shelves, trophies, and plaques. Jacob stared more at Pete than at his office.

"Where's that black thing you usually have on your face?" Jacob asked. He gestured the shape of an L along his chin.

Pete paused. "Oh, you mean my headset," he said, laughing. "I really don't wear it that often."

"What's it for?" Jacob asked.

"I use it to talk to the other coaches during the game."

"Oh, so they can help you win?" Jacob asked.

"Yeah," Pete said. "I need a lot of help with that."

Stopping at a poster-sized photo, an aerial view of the USC-Michigan game at the Rose Bowl from the year before, Pete said,

"Jacob, see that tiny little speck right there?" He was pointing at the USC sideline, the players antlike.

"Yeah. I see it," Jacob said, looking closely.

"That's me," Pete said. "Can you believe it? Look how small I am."

Jacob squinted, getting closer to the photo. "That's you?"

"Yep. That's me."

Pete walked over to his desk, sat down, and autographed a photo for Jacob.

"The Trojans need you!" it said. "Fight On!"

I liked that. He gave Jacob a hug.

I hugged Pete and thanked him. Jacob crawled back into his stroller and held his football like an infant cradled in his arms. The miracle that Angelica started, Pete Carroll finished.

When I'd left the house that day, I was simply hoping for normalcy, the kind kids who are not sick have. From my perspective, the best I could do was make it to a museum after the busloads of germ laden school kids departed so we'd have the whole place to ourselves, that and a bottle of disinfecting hand gel; and I supposed we could let the good times roll.

We still made it to the Science Center to see the bug display. After that, Jacob and Mona snuggled up in the back seat, and I started driving home.

As so often happened on long quiet drives, I began to digest the events that marked this throw-up day where I had started out feeling angry at being the world's emesis basin. I hadn't known the bigger picture. I realized that I wasn't the one sitting in the skybox barking orders. In everyday life, I was just a speck standing on the sidelines in an arena filled with people just like me, doing our best to hear our coach's voice over the din of hollering and gnashing of teeth as games played on and spectators watched, waiting to see who would win and who would lose.

Lisa Solis DeLong

Two Fairy Wands

Working with families at the MHF was my all-time favorite job. I loved talking with parents and visiting children in their homes. I was glad to not have the responsibility of patient care. I loved planning and attending events where my responsibility was to meet and greet families. Some were already familiar to me from attending support group, and others were new to cancer and to the MHF. I understood their repulsion from these events and their confusion over how they ended up in this saddest of sad clubs in the first place. I understood their need for some sense of control and their fear of belonging to our fellowship.

I met Elizabeth Hill at support group that first year. I didn't know then that Jacob's cancer was coming. Her parents, Michael and Emily, sat in the circle with moms and dads baring their souls about chemo and misdiagnosis and shock, while the kids—Mike, Elizabeth, Matt, and Baby Danny—played in the kid's room with Candye Rucker. I liked this family from the first time I met them. Big brother Mikey reminded me of Justin—his handsome smile, bright eyes, and his constant concern over Elizabeth. "Here,

Elizabeth. Here's your pen," or, "I'll get that for you, Elizabeth." He loved his little, four-year-old sister. Everyone did. She was feisty and funny and ruled the room like the little queen she was. Sometimes she'd come to support group wearing fairy wings and tiaras, always in command. Once, she even declared that March 25 would be an international holiday.

"It's Happy Fancy Rainbow Day," she said in her sweet, squeaky voice, without missing a syllable. And we believed her.

But Elizabeth's battle against the rare acinar cell cancer, which had destroyed her pancreas, was neither fancy nor happy.

While Elizabeth's cancer was taking its toll on her tiny body, Jacob's diagnosis hit, causing Jacob to change from sibling visitor to cancer patient.

He knew Elizabeth from support group so when Jacob began treatments at the outpatient hematology-oncology unit, the one perk was that we would run into the Hill family. He always smiled when we found them on clinic days. Once, when we were there, Jacob and Elizabeth shared a space in the day hospital. Elizabeth had already had surgery to remove her pancreas, gallbladder, and spleen, most of her liver, and even part of her bowels. Elizabeth was a walking, talking, energetic phenomenon beyond any I had ever known.

The day hospital was full when Mike and Emily wheeled her through the door in her pink umbrella stroller. Frail and thin, she needed an infusion of some kind, and Jacob and I were happy to invite them behind our curtain. Caregivers hovered, trying to stay composed as stress levels rose in such cramped quarters. The shrill beeps of monitors, the ring of telephones, and constant TV chatter; still, we laughed, ate lunch, and watched *The Incredibles*. Elizabeth made it a party, the nurses—ever professional, ever upbeat—our hosts. But all parties must come to an end.

"Elizabeth?"

"Yes, Mommy?" she whispered.

"I love you so much."

"I love you too, Mommy," she said, closing her eyes.

"You are my only daughter, and I'm so glad you were given to me." Emily held her tight.

"Me too," Elizabeth said, becoming weaker from speaking. And then she sighed the most powerful words I have ever heard: "I had to wait such a long time for you, Mommy. You took such a long time."

Emily was stunned.

"Elizabeth? What do you mean you waited for me?"

"In heaven, Mommy," she whispered faintly. "I waited in heaven for you until you were ready."

When Elizabeth began to die, which happened at home, slowly, over a period of weeks, Emily had the wisdom to listen to what her precious only daughter had to say.

In the dark, wee hours of the morning, Elizabeth left her home while in her mother's arms.

I had attended many memorial services while working for the MHF. I'd asked Dave to come with me to Elizabeth's, but he declined. I felt lonely and afraid to go alone. Jacob was several months past his VOD episode, her death hit too close to home, and I felt compelled to attend. I stood in my kitchen and prayed, *Lord, please send someone to go with me to this one. I can't go alone.*

Jojo walked in and said, "Mom, can I go with you to Elizabeth's memorial?"

I hadn't expected that someone to be my fourteen-year-old daughter. At Elizabeth's memorial, people reflected on how precious their time was with her. Jojo sat next to me, holding my hand as we sat in the wooden pew, tears rolling off of our cheeks and as she handed me a tissue, I knew that she too had been chosen for me.

Reflecting on Elizabeth's life, with Jojo holding my hand, I remembered visiting Elizabeth one day after she had been sent home on hospice care. As I entered the living room, the sound of SpongeBob came from the TV, an attempt at entertaining her brothers. Visitors came in and out of the house, the screen door slammed each time as though it were a bustling Sunday barbeque. I didn't know if I could do it, see Elizabeth, without falling apart and adding to the chaos. Mike and Emily did their best to make me feel welcome in the midst of trying to comfort their daughter. "Do you need another pillow? More pain medicine?" they asked her in turn.

She was lying on her bed, a pink Cinderella bedspread crumpled at her feet. Her nearly bald head rested on her pillow. A few wisps of blonde hair still rooted just above her forehead lay across its surface. She was fidgety and wanted to be held. She sat up and crawled onto my lap for a little while, the weight of her body so light, like a small bag of twigs gathered from plum trees in the fall, only softer. It was a privilege to hold her so close; but the moment did not last, and her pain prevaled, leading her over to her mother's arms instead.

"I want to draw you something," she said, suddenly lifting her heavy head like baby bird fresh from its shell.

"Okay. If you feel up to it," I replied, glancing at Emily for approval.

Emily handed her a drawing tablet and crayons; and she began to draw, breathing heavily and sighing between strokes.

"It's a fairy," she said in her signature squeak as she drew a picture of a winged creature in glistening purple and pink, her favorite colors. Putting down her glitter crayon and flopping over on the couch, she handed it to me.

"She is so beautiful. Thank you, Elizabeth," I said, studying her work of art.

"I gave you two magic fairy wands." She pointed out each one with her delicate fingers. "See. There is one in this hand and one in that hand."

I leaned close. "Oh, that is so nice, Elizabeth. I've never seen a fairy with so many wands. Why did you give her two?"

Cocking her head up, she said, "Because you need extra power," sitting up and pointing at me as though she had her own invisible wand clenched in her hand, sending out splashes of silvery sparkle, bestowing a power on me I could not see with my eyes but felt to the depth of my heart.

"Thank you, Miss Elizabeth," I said, my throat tightening and my eyes becoming wet.

Remembering this tender moment at her funeral, I was glad to have Jojo to hold close.

A few days later, I had to take Jacob to CHLA for his routine maintenance treatment. I missed seeing Elizabeth and wanted her there with us. In a moment of troubled thinking, while Jacob winced at getting poked and prodded, I felt jealous of Elizabeth; it was a sick I-don't-want-to-do-this-anymore kind of jealous. I was that tired.

This is how it is when your child has cancer and there are no certainties that their treatment will work. Sometimes, you just want out. Elizabeth was stronger than me. She taught me that sometimes, while traveling on life's highway, even though it can get dark, we can still give off a little light even at the end.

Lisa Solis DeLong

Rats

Jacob's meltdowns came less frequently, ever since his new friend, Patty May, a black-and-white, sable-eyed rat, was introduced to his bedtime routine. Jessica took Jacob to the pet shop the week before. She was leaving for Berkeley the next day and wanted to get him something special before she left.

"Mom, can I get Jacob a rat?" she'd asked. "Remember Whiskers? She was a good rat." She reminisced about the rodent that kept her company when she was Jacob's age. A female, soft and smart, she had been good companion. Jessica was born independent and adventurous. I did not feel worried about her move. She had street smarts. I think I felt a certain amount of relief that she could escape Jacob's bedtime crying episodes, which had been escalating for months.

It could have been the severe bloody nose that triggered this one; the one that occurred when we were driving home from Uncle Ken's house in Palmdale, thirty miles from home and blood started pouring out of Jacob's nostril. Jojo applied pressure in the back seat but became exasperated, "Mom, come back here. There's a lot of blood."

I crawled into the backseat, grabbed a hospital basin and towel, which I still kept handy for vomit, and applied as much pressure as I could to Jacob's nose. The stain on the towel grew, and the bottom of the basin was already a half-inch deep in dark red blood.

"Drive straight to CHLA," I instructed Dave.

We pulled up to the ambulance entrance, I jumped out with Jacob, and a security guard grabbed a wheelchair. He gagged when he saw the soaked towel and blood-filled basin. All I could think was that the leukemia was back and that he was bleeding out. I knew he was losing a significant amount of blood. I remembered the training I'd received as a nurse where red Jell-O was used to simulate post-partum bleeding. Jacob's blood loss would have qualified as a hemorrhage.

That night, the ER team dropped everything and had accessed his port and had lab results in what seemed like minutes. They showed that his platelets were low but not enough to cause that kind of bleeding. His nosebleed was a result of a vessel in his nose, a normal reason. His leukemia had not returned. The bleeding stopped. We were exhausted.

Dave and I had been letting Jacob sleep with us, fearful that he would sleep through a nosebleed. Four months later, it was time to cut the cord.

"I feel sorry for you guys," Jessica had said as the nightly frustration of trying to get Jacob to sleep alone in his room peaked.

I hadn't fully expected the rat trick to work, but having Patty May with him, his light on, and the door closed, had helped him through the night all week. Jessica was right. Patty May was good company too.

It wasn't long ago that Jacob cried regularly, to the point of exhaustion, beginning at his nine-o'clock bedtime and ending close to midnight.

"I miss JD," he'd sob. "I want to go to heaven to see JD." And then one night, in the middle of an all-out cry, he wailed, "I want to be like JD! JD is all light, and I am only half light and half darkness."

Blood Brothers

He cried and shook and whimpered until he had nothing left, until his little, eight-year-old body, mind, and spirit were cried out. Then he'd fall asleep. Lying next to him, I could do nothing but listen, listen and stroke his soft, tan arm as he raised it to cover his face.

There wasn't much else to do when he cried about the brother he never knew. He had to make sense of having the same illness that took his brother's life at fifteen and threatened to do the same to him. I listened to him, too stunned to cry, too experienced to try and fix it, to make the tears go away. There must be tears in a life like this. How could there not? Leukemia lived on, consuming lives like a snake in a jungle attracted to the scent of blood. It would continue to find its next victim and squeeze the life out of it. Living in the shadow of death was not easy. Even an eight-year-old knows that. So we cried when it got tough, and we cried when we were tired, and we cried when we missed Justin.

Lying there in the company of my finally quiet, little champion, I heard the sound of my heart beating and thought back to when I was a little girl, close to Jacob's age. I'd lie awake at night, tucked in neatly within the sheets of the top bunk of the set I shared with my little sister, who had the bottom. Every night, I would inch carefully between the sheets, slipping in like a letter into an envelope, so as not to mess the sheets and blankets. *Who wants to make a bed every day?* I thought. Waking each morning, I'd slide out delicately, pull the top of the sheets, and voila! My bed was made. My older sister, asleep on the twin bed next to us, would be sprawled across her bed, sheets hanging on the floor, pillow over her head, looking more like a pile of dirty laundry than a person sleeping. She'd look up at me slithering out of my neatly laid bed and give me a look of complete disgust, like sisters tend to do at that age.

Our bedroom was what would be considered small by today's standards. In my memory, it was large, expansive, and kind of scary. Very often, when the three of us lay there at night, my mind would drift to the place between wakefulness and sleep, and I would hear it—the loud, pounding steps of what I believed was a giant coming down the street to pluck me out of the safety of my bed. Louder and louder the thumping would increase, and I would begin to tremble. Pulling the sheets, blankets, and bedspread up over my head, the footsteps came closer and closer. In my mind, I could see it, large and dark, at least the size of the fruited mulberry tree I'd climbed in the front yard that day. Holding my breath, I'd lie there, contemplating screaming but fearful of waking my sisters. Faster and faster the footsteps came. Louder and louder until eventually I'd fall asleep.

I don't know exactly when it happened, but I distinctly remember when the giant stopped visiting. I was there in my usual place among my sisters one night, when after the bedtime chatter had subsided and the room became quiet, the footsteps began. This time, I noticed a familiar pattern to the giant's footsteps. As the adrenaline pumped through my body, the pounding sounded even more recognizable. I don't know why I hadn't distinguished it sooner; but that night, in my straightjacket of a bed, I realized the sound that had been terrifying me for weeks, possibly even months, was not the sound of a giant wishing to harm me. Rather, it was the sound of my own heartbeat.

It seemed so obvious, so ridiculous, that the *lub-dub, lub-dub* of my own heart could be the source of one of the most frightening experiences of my youthful life. I felt foolish and relieved and never shared this experience with anybody. How could I have been so afraid of something so palpable? What I feared was the thing that gave me life.

In what felt like a hundred years since Justin's original diagnosis, I knew that I was not a victim of a cold and distant giant wishing to punish me but rather a willing participant in a pre-calculated plan involving children who were well-equipped for their earthbound journey before they ever agreed to enter my womb.

When I found myself weary from Jacob's crying, drifting into thoughts about life and death, as I looked into his soggy-eyelash eyes and wondered if he would be plucked away from me, my heart began to beat faster and my neck thickened and the fear began to mess up this neat little place of respite I had managed to wrap myself in most days, a place of living, loving, and joy. Rising to tears, I recognized the excruciating throb of fear; and I wanted to hide, make it go away. And then, in a moment of desperate prayer and petition to please not make me do this again—live without another one of my children—the déjà-vu of chemo and suffering whizzed around my mind, messy emotions attached to this life of day-to-day laying down and waking up to the same fears and realities that were mine; and then a calm as I recognized the sound, the sound of my own heart, a mother's heart, and I realized that this giant had stared at me before. *We're all going to die someday,* I'd think to myself. *There's no surprise in that, no sneaking around in the dark about that anymore.*

The tears flowed, the fear subsided, and I knew in my heart of hearts that whether Jacob lived to be fifteen or fifty, when he died, his brother would be there to greet him. Whether Jacob remained in this world or the other, this was my life's path, the one which my creator and I reviewed before I was born.

Nighttimes were like this sometimes—thoughts visited and lessons were learned.

"Did JD like rats?" Jacob asked after one of his crying episodes.

"Yes. JD liked rats," I replied.

"They are very smart, aren't they?" he continued.

"Yes. Rats are very smart," I agreed.

"How long do rats live?" he wondered aloud as his eyes began to close.

"As long as rats are supposed to live," I whispered.

Jacob sniffled and sputtered a post-crying kind of sigh, like children do when their tears have finally quieted them. He exhaled, breathing deeply, each breath a little slower, a little more peaceful. We lay there in his twin-sized bed, eyes closed, his legs wrapped around mine, our arms entwined like vines. Patty May took a trip on her hamster wheel. Around and around she ran. We fell asleep as the wheel turned and tapped against the transparent walls of her sturdy glass cage.

De-Ported

Jacob was being de-ported. His central line, which had been surgically placed three years and four months prior for treatment purposes, was no longer needed. Dave and Jacob and I were in the waiting room at an outpatient surgery center in San Fernando. This was where our medical group, the great and powerful Oz of providers, had sent Jacob to have his port removed. You wouldn't know it that day, but I love our medical group. They had taken care of every need, first with Justin then with Jacob. He had received top-notch care, the best in the country by most standards. But that day, I was like a spoiled child. I hadn't gotten my way. I wanted Jacob's port removed at CHLA because it was home to us. I didn't know anybody here in the waiting room filled with men and women who looked like my great aunts and uncles. There were no children here except Jacob. That made me nervous.

I hated waiting, but having Dave at my side helped. I asked him what had changed since we did all of this the first time, and he said, "I was so afraid of losing Justin back then that I got lost in running. I really think Justin and I grew up together."

He was right. I appreciated his silver hair, his tan, weathered face, and his honesty—a handsome testament to his age. The door to the waiting room swung open, and a nurse speaking in airline-stewardess fashion directed us to follow her.

"Sit here, Jacob. Put this on, Jacob. What is that, Jacob? Drink this, Jacob ... "

It was not her fault that she seemed overzealous and much too cheerful. She spoke in a loud voice as if she were talking to old people. She had said her name so many times that I wondered if I would ever forget it. My irritability was to blame. She was thorough and professional, but when her very detailed explanations of what would happen next made Jacob's eyes bulge, mother bear started to come out of her cave, and I wanted to take a swipe at her.

"Jacob, do you know why you are here?" the nurse asked.

"Uh, to take out my port," he said in such a soft voice I could barely hear him.

As her explanations increased, so did his anxiety. Some kids don't need a lot of information.

He began to tear.

Dave noticed the tension mounting in me and Jacob and opened the new LEGO set he brought to keep Jacob busy while he was waiting to have his skin sliced open and the thing he had relied on to make him well removed. Jacob focused on the set and smiled. He opened each bag of square and rectangular pieces and began building his masterpiece.

Just as he was getting lost in his creation, the nurse returned with a "cocktail" of Verced and Tylenol; Jacob did not want to take it. He didn't want to get groggy. He never got a "cocktail" at CHLA when he went under. Not the first time and not the fourteenth time. LEGOS were far more powerful than Verced or Tylenol at calming his nerves. All he wanted was to build his LEGO set, which was what we did when we were waiting to go under anesthesia.

The anesthesiologist walked up and said, "My boys play with LEGOS too."

But Jacob wasn't just playing. He was escaping.

The doctor made good eye contact and was calm. "I'm going to give you some medicine in your IV soon to help you sleep."

"The white medicine?" Jacob asked.

"Yes. Propofol."

They had used Propofol at CHLA every time.

We calmed down.

"Go ahead and drink the cocktail now. It will help you to feel better when you wake up."

Jacob drank the bright red syrup and shuddered at the taste.

I knew he could handle Propofol and that he would cry when he started to go under. He didn't like how it felt to lose consciousness, which was what happened next. And he was wheeled away on a gurney, doped up as he passed through the double doors again. As we put away the LEGOS, I tried not to cry. This was supposed to be a happy moment where the catheter that was put there to pump toxic chemicals into his veins to keep him alive was no longer needed. But as Jacob—my gentle Jacob—entered the other room, I thought about how he continued to teach me new perspectives on life and death and the color of the sky and the invisible nearness of his brother, JD. How he reminded me to look for the artful details found in everyday life, like the tiny intricacy of the black lines found on butterfly wings only noticeable if you look close.

He pulled me in to the here and the now, much like he had when he was a toddler, and had slapped me across the face. I recalled the day he asked if we could make chocolate-covered strawberries because they were "so beautiful and chocolaty and smooth." All he could think about then was food—buying it, making it, and eating it.

After eating three of his strawberry creations, he had asked, "Can we go for a walk? Then make tortilla soup?" He couldn't stop thinking about food when he was on decadron. At the same time he wanted to get his head out of the refrigerator because he was tired of eating. I remembered when he used to get bloated, when what made him feel better was to go outdoors so he could see the sky and the "beautiful sunset."

He had sucked me in to the sweet taste of motherhood whenever he created elephants and dinosaurs out of clay from his bare hands in a matter of seconds and they had looked like they could come to life and run off the table and bellow.

On that gurney he was tan, green-eyed, and adorable, and he made me love living with him here on planet earth more each day.

It was good to be done with his port; but even after doing this so many times, I was not okay with seeing him carted away by strangers who were even stranger than usual because they were not my CHLA nurses, anesthesiologists, and surgeons. These people were for big people, not little people; and the whole thing was freaking me out.

Dave and I held each other, our eyes wet. Once again, Jacob was on the other side.

I hated waiting.

I had told the pre-op nurse that Jacob would like to keep his port, to which she replied, "Oh, I don't think that will be possible."

I had asked the OR nurse too, because I was not going to give up on the idea, and besides, I knew kids at CHLA who had kept their ports.

And I told her, "My other son got to keep his."

I had to play all my cards. This nurse said that she had worked at CHLA too and knew that they didn't allow it there either.

"It is pretty gunky when it comes out, and there is no way for us to autoclave it."

Sometimes I wondered if medical personnel forgot to speak in lay terms or if they did it on purpose just to shut people up. This nurse did not know that I spoke her language.

Wouldn't it be more appropriate to say, "Sterilize"? *If I ever go back to work, I will speak to people in terms they can understand.*

These poor nurses. I was just looking for a fight. I didn't trust them. I hadn't had time. Our pre-op nurse returned and talked too fast and too loud as she directed us to the waiting room.

"Follow the carpeted floor on your way out. If you follow the linoleum, we might end up doing surgery on you."

Now there's a confidence builder.

She had irritated the crap out of me. I left for the bathroom.

Did I mention that I hated waiting?

It was supposed to be fifteen minutes. Now it was thirty, and all I could think about was the long list of risk factors the surgeon defined for me at out pre-op meeting, the one where I had tried to talk him into approving our request to have the port removed at CHLA because the last time Jacob went under anesthesia for a lumbar puncture, he ended up with an aspiration pneumonia that presented itself about an hour after he was discharged from the recovery room and landed him on Four East for three days. Thanks to the quick work of the oncology team there, it was diagnosed on the spot and treated aggressively and all was well. This was how it was with Jacob. It took a team.

I had used all of the techniques I could think of to convince the man to give in. I went from a sitting to a standing position when we talked. I moved closer to him and puffed up my chest like a mother hen. I looked him directly in the eyes. I told him about the pnuemo and my other son. I told him I was a nurse and that I had seen too much.

He went on to explain the risks and made the mistake of saying, "It is very rare, but ... "

If we had been talking about steaks that would have been fine, but we weren't. As he ran down the list of potential problems, including *respiratory failure* and *intubation*, if he had known how many times those words "very rare" had entered my ears only to become reality, surely he would have agreed to have the procedure done at CHLA. If he had known how "rare" we were, he'd probably have paid us *not* to come to his surgical center. But nothing worked, and here we were.

So I sat in the room for waiting next to Dave, and I began a silent prayer.

Lord, help my boy and all the employees whom I think have only seen what is normal, what is common in this outpatient surgical center for big people. Bless the anesthesiologist. Bless Jacob. Bless the annoying nurse who told Jacob to pick a plastic ducky while we were waiting and did it with such gusto that it scared him.

"Here. This one is a pirate ducky. Or you could pick the soldier or the angel ducky or a…"

She talked so fast and so forcefully that Jacob, who spoke slowly like JD had, but had the unique ability to develop ten questions for every one scenario presented to him, finally stopped her and asked, "Mom, what are they for?" He didn't understand why she was forcing rubber duckies down his throat at a time like this. He wasn't taking a bath.

"Are they for me to bite on or something?"

I pictured surgery in the Old West when a dusty cowboy was given a piece of leather to clamp his teeth on to keep him from screaming.

I pictured Jacob biting down on a yellow rubber ducky.

The addressograph slid across another patient's plastic identification card as we sat in the waiting room.

I hated waiting.

Perhaps I needed a rubber ducky.

Finally "DeLong, Jacob" was called, and Dave and I jumped up and made our way to the recovery room. His favorite bright, red pillow stood out like a drop of blood on a white gauze pad. Jacob was pale, but his lips were pink, the peaceful rise and fall of his chest beneath his bright orange leopard print blanket was a sure sign he was asleep. That blanket had accompanied him to all of his surgical procedures. I brought it on purpose so I could identify him quickly among the generic rows of white gurneys bearing some other mother's sleeping child. The days of wildcat recoveries had subsided somewhere between anesthesia three and five and so, as we had with Justin, we held his hand and watched him recover.

His port was sitting at the bottom of a specimen container on the bedside table. A white dome the size of a bottle cap anchored a thin tail that was the catheter itself. A piece of Jacob's red tissue remained attached to the top of the tail, giving the whole thing a jellyfish-like appearance. It curved to the confines of the jar and looked like one of those deep-sea creatures that never developed eyes for lack of light.

For three and a half years, it had been in the dark recesses of Jacob's body, serving faithfully to keep him alive.

I felt teary when I saw the gauze taped over the port site.

The bump under his skin was gone.

The port had served Jacob well, and it was difficult for me to grasp the idea that he didn't need it anymore. Now, when Jacob had a fever, we would not have to rush to CHLA's ER for antibiotics and blood work. No more "protecting the port" as we had been told over and over again.

We had crossed the border into a new country. We had made it over the fence, past the barbed wire, and we were back to our native land. There was no going back! Do you hear me? No going back!

The nurse here in the recovery room was much more soft spoken. I told her the whole story about Justin and Jacob and their cancers. I told her about Jacob finding Justin's Hickman catheter in a Ziploc bag in my dresser drawer.

"This was JD's, wasn't it?" he'd asked one day while looking for a bandana.

Her eyes teared.

Jacob was the only child in the recovery room. I told her how the pre-op nurse said, "No" to keeping the port; how the surgical nurse said, "No"; and how the surgeon said, "No."

As Jacob slept for two and a half hours and Dave rested his eyes in the recliner, we talked, and she heard me.

"I'll write a note on the lab slip." She took her pen and wrote, "Please do not discard. Patient will pick up port." It was a simple, silent gesture.

That afternoon, at 3:30, my cell phone rang.

"Mrs. DeLong?" a female voice questioned.

"Yes."

"This is Maria from the lab at Holy Cross."

"Yes."

"I have your son's portacath ready. You can pick it up anytime."

"What? That's great! What happened? How come we get to keep it?"

"I saw the request written on the lab slip and showed it to the pathologist. He said, 'That poor kid. He has probably been to hell and back with that thing. Of course he can have it.'"

Finally, a sympathetic human being who understood a little boy's need to keep his trophy, the one tangible thing that symbolized his leukemia and his ability to defeat it.

That night, we went straight to the gym, where Jojo was playing basketball. Jacob took the sterilized port out of its container and asked anyone who would listen, "Want to see my port?" And then, holding it by the tail like it was a scorpion, he brought it closer and grinned as he watched the spectators wince.

Dancing On a Trap Door

In the spring of 2010, I was driving Jacob to a school for homeschoolers three days a week. One morning had started like this: "Jacob, brush your teeth. Jacob, get your coat. Jacob, grab your lunch." And then, as we pulled up to the front of the school, "Did you bring your backpack?"

"Didn't you get it, Mom?" he asked as he sucked down the last of his Ovaltine milk drink and I parked.

I got out of the car and looked in the backseat. Welling with frustration, I said, "It is your backpack, not mine. See that? That's my purse. I remembered it. Your backpack is *yours*. You have to remember it."

It was lab result day, where a vial no bigger than a man's finger held Jacob's future, and I was edgy. The fourth week of every month, I held my breath as the horror of the past teetered on the present. Our family lived with a kind of heart-stopping PTSD—post-traumatic stress disorder—where our anxiety peeked high over seemingly benign incidents. Like one of Jacob's bloody nose episodes, for instance. Lots of kids had them, but when Jacob did and we ran for a pile of tissues, we shuddered at the memories associated with the more than twenty ER visits it had taken to keep him alive.

Every day carried the possibility of relapse. The problem with lab days was that the vial of Jacob's blood dangling in my face magnified normal daily stresses. I felt like it could slip any second and bring my world crashing to the ground, leaving us shattered and bloodied.

Jacob had been off of chemotherapy for eight months. The three-and-a-half-year season of adverse side effects was over. Eight months of no mood swings, no muscle aches, no bloating, and no fatigue. His hair was thicker, softer, and shinier. His caterpillar eyebrows had crawled back onto his face and given him the frame they were intended to give. His dark eyelashes made his green eyes appear greener. His lips were as red as grapes and just as soft and sweet. He kissed me time and again, little boy pecks of love for a mommy who was smiling more and laughing often. The remnant spider veins on his cheeks—the kind associated with old men who drank too much—were slowly disappearing. His sandpaper skin was now supple.

That morning as Jacob and I had made the ten mile trip to his school, the road curved and took us past Beale's Cut, where Justin and I had once walked with his sixth-grade class, the first of the slices through the Newhall Pass where a general lead a team of soldiers and Chinese laborers with pickaxes and shovels to slash through a mountain. I reminisced about how Justin and I wore our hiking shoes and padded our way through the narrow, sandy path on my left. When we had held hands that day, we could almost touch both sides of the cut at the same time. The site was closed now. The walls had caved but not the memories.

As I drove, a Big Band song blasted through the car stereo and took me back to 1998's swing dance class with Justin. He had offered to take Dave's place a few weeks in to the lessons, and I was glad he had. When his leukemia returned a year later, there was no room for dancing.

I turned a corner and felt butterflies in my stomach as I thought about the dance lesson I had scheduled for that afternoon. A few months prior, I had volunteered to dance the cha-cha to raise funds for the Michael Hoefflin Foundation for Children's Cancer. The organizers of the event had paired me by height with professional ballroom instructor Richard Pearce, a small man with a big heart who volunteered to teach me. Other than that brief swing class, I'd had no training.

As I drove, I thought about the week before the fundraising performance. Dancing with Richard had made me recall how good it felt to dance with Justin. I had struggled to make sense of the euphoria I felt. The physical memory of my son's touch had resurrected. I'd lived with grief long enough to know that another painful layer had to be peeled back. At that time my heart ached, and my chest hurt. I knew then that I needed to have a massive cry. I'd gone to Justin's grave, where I had always done my best crying, and sat in my car. As soon as I turned on the stereo, the song "Cats in the Cradle" played. By the time I heard the first, "When you comin' home son, I don't know when…," I'd lost it. My shoulders rose and fell, my head slumped forward between my hands on the steering wheel, and I heaved giant, sorrowful sobs. My soul hurt, and the pain had needed out.

This was what happiness did to me—not because I didn't think I deserved it. If anyone deserved a little sunshine, I thought it was me. But when life was good, really, really good, it made me miss Justin in the worst way. I wanted him here.

That morning, with Jacob at my side, I felt the edges of my mouth rise to honor the memory of receiving all "8's" at the fundraising event and Jacob running up to me saying, "I would have given you all 10's, Mom!" as I walked off the floor. Life was so full of twists and turns, and this one had taken me so far away from my sickness-filled life that sometimes I felt like I was getting pretty good at my dance with death.

After I became proficient with the cha-cha, I wanted to learn more dances. I had asked Richard to teach me social ballroom dancing, to which he had agreed. The first time I went social dancing was a stretch. Having developed a non-family-related hobby was one thing but walking out the door on a weeknight was another. I had been feeling uneasy about venturing out by myself that night. But when Dave had said, "Aren't you going dancing with Richard tonight?" he said it in the same voice he used when one of his athletes needed encouragement. "You should go. Call him and go."

All I could think of then was, *What planet have I landed on? What kind of life is this that I am living, in this wonderful, amazing, freedom-filled world where my children are healthy and my husband says, "Go dance with another man"?*

That night I had paid a ten-dollar fee to enter Ballroom By The Bay at the Santa Monica Women's Club. A woman in a red chiffon dress had greeted Richard and let him in for free because he was a teacher there and, at the age of sixty-one, was a seasoned veteran. I had felt proud to be associated with someone carrying enough clout to have earned a feeless entry and nervous that I might disappoint him. We walked through a tall, thick doorway and entered a grand Art Deco style room with two-story-high ceilings and windows reaching from eye level to sky level and a ceiling adorned with white lights draped like pearl necklaces. Pillars rose reminding me of stilettos. The ballroom floor was encircled by couples in hold, preparing for promenade. Music tinkled light and elegant as a group of beautiful, gray-haired men and women meandered. It seemed that they, unlike me, had done this a thousand times.

I had butterflies.

I took Richard's hand, and he directed me to a standing hold the way we had practiced. He knew I needed a warm-up, and he said "Slow, slow, quick, quick," in my ear. We swayed starting to my right, and then again, "Slow, slow, quick, quick. Here we go." And we were off, and I was dancing, really dancing—the kind of dancing I'd only seen in 1950's movies, where elegant women with long, white necks glided across smooth dance floors in soft, crepe dresses and diamond necklaces. I was fox trotting.

At one of my lessons, with Richard, he had said, "Every dance must have a leader and a follower. Without this dynamic, dancing would be chaotic and without foundation." He had become frustrated with me on several occasions when I'd lost concentration, relaxed my arms and let my frame get weak. He shook my wrist and repeated, "Frame. I need a frame. I can't lead you without it." My faith was like that too. Believing in God more as a partner and less as a dictator gave me structure. Trusting that he knew what he was doing, even if the steps I had to learn felt awkward and left me with blisters, gave me a sense of cohesiveness most of the time.

In my royal blue and black, rayon, tea-length dress, every nerve ending was on high alert. I was sashaying, swaying, and moving to the right and to the left. I felt light and airy and ultra feminine, which was rare in my world of mother, wife, and caregiver.

I was so happy I hardly recognized myself.

When I crawled into bed that night and rubbed my sore feet against Dave's warm, muscular legs, all I could think about was how much he loved me and how good it felt to be in bed with him back in our sanctuary.

More often than not, when I drove Jacob to school, fox trot and hustle steps had taken up the floor space in my mind. But memories like the time when the phone woke me at 3:00 a.m. "Jacob's lab results are abnormal," the doctor had said in a sleepy voice. "You need to take him to CHLA immediately." My heart had hit the pit of my stomach, and I'd felt nauseous only to find out hours later that it had all been a mistake.

On lab days, when memories like that made their way to center stage, I felt like I was dancing on a trap door.

Still on our way, I wove between a Honda and a semi as the road descended beneath the overpass of the 14 and 5 Freeways. Two men in bright, orange hardhats held signs saying, "Caution! Prepare to

Stop." The flagman flipped the stop sign and gestured to proceed. A tangle of concrete and steel weaved overhead like massive tentacles connecting one mountainous pinnacle to another, releasing Los Angeles-bound commuters every day. Jacob and I had watched this new construction process all year.

"Mom, tell me about the earthquake again."

He liked hearing about the '94 Northridge earthquake. We drove under the section that had fallen apart back then where a motorcycle cop fell through the gap. Jacob saw every detail and would likely sketch it later. He saw the world with an artistic morbid eye.

"It is so big? How far did he fall?" he asked, looking up.

Jacob and I traveled beneath spires of steel and concrete balancing on what looked like metal building blocks, reminding me more of his LEGO creations than a freeway. Steel pipes the size of trains littered the roadside, and men in white hardhats dangled from pylons.

Often, as I ventured closer to Jacob's school and thoughts of Justin lingered, I was taken by the extreme divergence of the landscape. Dry cliffs cut, stripped, and weather beaten had little foliage below the lush terrain of blue sage, scrub oak, and heritage oaks above. Even so, it was the cliff-hanging clusters of peach orange flowers dangling their snapdragon faces that impressed me the most. I thought of how tough it must have been for those delicate plants to thrive with so little to hold onto.

I loved this time of year—the cool, spring morning still affording me the pleasure of slurping coffee hot from my favorite blue mug and piling on my soft, white, down comforter for the chill of night. Spring season had sprung with such intensity this year that the foliage surrounding us was so green I swear I could taste it.

It seemed like ten years of winter, including the death of my father and David's mother, had sprung into a phenomenal season of new life. I had the odd but familiar sense that I had come to a clearing just like the one in my recurring freeway dream, when all the chaotic crashes have stopped.

Blood Brothers

An unprecedented array of dreams had blossomed before my eyes: healthy children, a thriving marriage, a new home, ballroom dancing, and an opportunity to work with other bereaved families— all of this in less than three months. Life was coming at me with so much vigor that I could barely take it all in. I found myself saying, "Thank you, Jesus. Thank you, Justin," over and over again. There was so much gratitude pouring out of me that I just had to say it. I wondered if this was how Job felt at the end of his story, when he made it to the good part, the one people rarely talk about, when he gets his life back and gets it back big.

As I drove I thought about Jessica and Jojo. Having a twenty-one-year-old and sixteen-year-old in the house had been, to my surprise, a great delight. They had traveled this road together through all the vomit, syringes, IV lines, and emergency room visits. They were just as much blood sisters as the boys were blood brothers. They had needed each other but hadn't always been able to express that need or receive each other's embrace. I'd noticed a melancholy spirit about them lately.

Just the other day we talked about what it was like when Justin had gotten sick, how Jessica remembered the morning of his relapse, me standing there, numb, as Papa sent them out the door.

"I remember yelling at you on our way to school, Jojo, because you kept asking me what was wrong, and I knew something bad had happened but I didn't know what it was so I told you to just shut up."

"I don't even remember that one. You must not have yelled at me too bad."

They laughed, and then I asked, "Here we are in the most beautiful home, being overdosed with blessings beyond our capacity to create for ourselves, with Jacob healed and everything being profoundly good. So why have we been so sad?"

And then my Jojo said, "Because everything has been about cancer for so long, and now it is gone, and everything is good, and all we can do is ask, 'What do we do now?'"

Jessica and I high-fived her.

Still driving that morning, Jacob and I passed Eternal Valley. I didn't like seeing it, and many times I had thought about going a different way, but that would have added twenty minutes to our commute. The quickest route was by the cemetery.

I remembered sitting there at Justin's grave with Jacob, being prickled by the grass and irritated by the wind, and I thought about the long stretches of disillusion that had taught me how to live without one son while embracing the privilege of living with the other.

As we drove by, I noticed Jacob's head turn in the direction of the enormous, wrought-iron gates of the cemetery. I wondered if he was thinking what I was thinking: *Will the leukemia come back? Will he relapse?* I didn't dare say the *R* word, but with every cough, runny nose, and sore throat, I thought it.

As we passed the cemetery, the question was, did he?

I asked him, "Jacob, what do you think about when we pass by here?"

"I don't know. About Justin, I guess." He shrugged.

I nodded, wondering if he was thinking about his own death someday. In his ten-year-old mind filled with animated images of dragons and dragon slayers, he asked, "Mom, is his body just bones now?" He made a wet, squishy sound with his mouth and wrinkled his fingers in waves as though he were mimicking skin slithering off of bone. He had been doing this since he was little, making sound effects.

"Yes. His body is just bones now." I drove, minding a curve in the road. I wanted to probe him for more, but I wouldn't do that to him.

I reached over and gave Jacob's knee a squeeze and said, "I love you, Jakie boy." I did this a lot when we were driving, half for the pleasure of feeling the strength in his leg and half to confirm that he was still there.

We took a hard right onto The Old Road and then to his school. Jacob and I got out of the car. My irritability over forgetting his backpack faded quickly as he stuffed a plastic baggy of sliced apples and a granola bar into his pockets. I put my arm around his shoulder as we walked to the front of the school. Wearing his black Fedora and torn-at-the-knee jeans, he looked too cute to stay mad at. I kissed his cheek and let my lips linger as I took in his puppy-like scent in a deep breath, wishing I could inhale him forever.

I got back in my car, left the parking lot, and began my way home when the phone rang. I recognized our pediatrician's number. I hesitated to answer. If it was the nurse's voice I heard on the other end of the phone, then I would know Jacob's labs were okay. If it was the doctor calling, it meant bad news, and I would need to pull over. I took a deep breath and answered. It was the nurse.

"Hello, may I speak to the parent of Jacob DeLong?"

"Yes, this is his mom."

"I just called to let you know that Jacob's labs are normal."

I exhaled and looked ahead at the purple blue flowers of black sage blanketing the mountainsides on either side of the pavement all around me. The road had opened wide, and I reveled in the hope of having another month of days this good.

Lisa Solis DeLong